Other

A New Approach to Counselling
and Listening Skills

First published by O Books, 2009
O Books is an imprint of John Hunt Publishing Ltd., The Bothy, Deershot Lodge, Park Lane, Ropley,
Hants, SO24 0BE, UK
office1@o-books.net
www.o-books.net

Distribution in:

UK and Europe
Orca Book Services
orders@orcabookservices.co.uk
Tel: 01202 665432 Fax: 01202 666219
Int. code (44)

USA and Canada
NBN
custserv@nbnbooks.com
Tel: 1 800 462 6420 Fax: 1 800 338 4550

Australia and New Zealand
Brumby Books
sales@brumbybooks.com.au
Tel: 61 3 9761 5535 Fax: 61 3 9761 7095

Far East (offices in Singapore, Thailand,
Hong Kong, Taiwan)
Pansing Distribution Pte Ltd
kemal@pansing.com
Tel: 65 6319 9939 Fax: 65 6462 5761

South Africa
Alternative Books
altbook@peterhyde.co.za
Tel: 021 555 4027 Fax: 021 447 1430

Text copyright Caroline Brazier 2008

Design: Stuart Davies

ISBN: 978 1 84694 191 7

A CIP catalogue record for this book is available
from the British Library.

Printed in the UK by CPI Antony Rowe, Chippenham, Wiltshire

O Books operates a distinctive and ethical publishing philosophy in
all areas of its business, from its global network of authors to
production and worldwide distribution.
This book is produced on FSC certified stock, within ISO14001
standards. The printer plants sufficient trees each year through
the Woodland Trust to absorb the level of emitted carbon in
its production.

Listening to the Other

A New Approach to Counselling
and Listening Skills

Caroline Brazier

BOOKS

Winchester, UK
Washington, USA

CONTENTS

To my mother, Jean Bates

who taught me the importance of common sense and a sense
of humour

Prologue

It was 1974 when I first attended a listening skills course. I was eighteen, and I rather suspect my attendance had more to do with the fact that my boyfriend of the time had signed up as a volunteer with the university Nightline service. Since I was rather shy of taking initiative in those days, I tagged along to the first training session, listened to a talk from the organiser of the service, an older student who seemed immensely mature to my fresh-out-of-school eyes, and joined in the listening exercises, which were done back to back in pairs, for this was a telephone counselling service.

Those early experiences convinced me that I liked listening to people. I was interested in their stories and delighted that they seemed to want to talk to me. Whether I was the listener, practising open-ended questions and sympathetic murmuring, or the caller, pouring out imagined troubles in role-play scenarios, the process of creating a shared space in which feelings could be aired and solace found was deeply satisfying. I became instantly convinced of the value of the listening ear and the space to talk. For the next four years I continued to volunteer with the service and eventually, as I became one of its more experienced members, began to train others in basic listening skills.

It was in the early eighties that I found myself once more involved in offering listening support. I was now a young mother with three small children. Twins had arrived two years after my first daughter. Life was hectic but myopic. As the initial phase of sleepless nights and nappies began to abate, I started to look around in the local community for new ways to engage with things beyond the confines of home. A circuitous process of voluntary committees and local networks brought me into contact with a group of women who were planning to create a women's health project on Tyneside.

This project, it turned out, was part of a wave of voluntary projects which opened on Tyneside in the early eighties. Those were exciting times. I soon found myself participating in a maze of voluntary sector groups, health groups, women's education groups and personal growth groups. I met lots of interesting, creative people. I explored the roots of social structures and attitudes. I learned that beneath the surface, personal history and beliefs drive our lives in all manner of unexpected ways. I discovered that human process was trustworthy, and that groups could endure terrible conflicts and come out stronger as a result. I learned to cry and laugh with others. I met people who inspired me and who, in turn, drew on their own sources of inspiration in the national and international movements of experimental growth groups and women's groups. All of this taught me new dimensions of listening.

As time went on, workshops gave way to courses and listening skills to counselling and groupwork training. I started to work as a therapist and for the past twenty years counselling and psychotherapy have been an important strand in my professional life. But the values I learned from those early groups did not alter. Nor have I lost my sense of the value of community groups, offering listening at grass roots level. I have always valued the immediacy and common sense groundedness of the voluntary project, the listening service and the drop-in centre, and have continued to work in such settings on and off through the years.

In the last year, our spiritual community opened a city centre drop-in in Leicester. We have started to train volunteers from different faith groups in basic listening skills, and these volunteers staff the drop-in. For the most part my involvement with this project is supportive. I offer supervision to those who are at the project's front line, and once again, I find myself teaching listening skills. Once again, I am in touch with the immediacy of the volunteer listener's position. This book has come out of this process. It is a book which draws together the simple, open hearted enthusiasm of the volunteer, and that fresh willingness to hear whatever people wish to talk about, with the experience of nearly thirty-five years in the field.

I have been listening for a long time. At the end of the day though, each time I sit down with a new visitor in our community, each time I visit a patient in the hospital where I now do chaplaincy work, each time somebody comes to me for a therapy session, the experience is new. My history is just a jumping off point. It has, if nothing else, given me faith that listening can and does make a difference to people. But, in truth, I know nothing. With the person who sits before me in any particular meeting, I have everything to learn, and only they can help me.

Notes on exercises

This is not a book which you can readily read on the bus or train. It requires you to engage in practical ways. As you go through the material it contains you will find a lot of exercises to help you integrate the learning which you are receiving. These exercises are the backbone of what is presented. Learning is an active process and this book offers a framework for developing skills. Although simply reading it will give you something, you will gain most from the process if you treat it as a study programme and use the suggested activities to explore and refine the skills which are being described.

GROUP AND SOLITARY LEARNING

Listening skills are generally taught in groups for obvious reasons. Listening requires at least two people, the speaker and the listener. If we are going to learn to listen, we need someone to listen to. Getting feedback on the quality of our listening and hearing what other people have noticed in the same story is an invaluable aid to learning. So, where it is possible, developing listening skills is best done with others. This book is therefore one which may be used by groups who wish to develop their skills together, working with a facilitator, or as a self-programming group of peers.

On the other hand, you may be one of the many people in helping professions who are trying to develop skills without having a group of people to work with. I have therefore presented most of the exercises in the book in forms that can be used by one person working on their own. Despite the obvious disadvantages of this solitary approach, this format should allow you to explore your skills and find ways to refine and develop them.

One of the advantages of working in this way is that you can proceed at your own pace. The book allows you to integrate your learning in your work context by spreading the study over time.

4

You can also go back to earlier sessions as relevant situations arise. This has some advantages over the standard one or two day 'Introduction to Listening Skills' course, which you might be offered, as it gives time for reflection, growth and for trying out skills in your regular work along the way.

One way of studying these skills on your own is through working in an on-line peer group. If you are interested in linking up with other people who are studying this programme to share experiences of the exercises, you can contact us at courses@amidatrust.com. We will put you in touch with others who are in the same position and offer a point of reference for your studies.

A few of the exercises included in the book are offered specifically for groups. Where this is the case, it is indicated on the exercise and an alternative is given. Mostly though, the exercises are presented in a form which you can do on your own. There are also some notes included which refer to working in groups. These are probably of interest to the solitary reader as well as to group members, for we all encounter groups from time to time, and, if you are working as a listener, you may well sometimes find yourself working in group situations.

If you are working in a group, you can use most of the exercises in the book as a basis for doing paired listening skills exercises, even though this is not generally indicated on the instructions. (To do so every time would be repetitious and unnecessary.) In most cases the exercises will work best if you start off by doing the activity individually and then work in pairs to share what you have learned, taking turns so that one person acts as the listener and the other as the speaker and then vice versa.

Alternative formats would involve:
- Working in groups of three, with the third person acting as observer and giving feedback to the listener on their facili-

tation skills (see the instructions in session three).

- Alternatively, each person might undertake the exercise individually and then share responses using a stone passing circle (see session one for a description of this method).

PRACTICALITIES

Many of the exercises given include drawing or writing. You will need lots of big sheets of paper, so you might like to invest in a child's drawing book, a flip chart or a roll of lining paper. Alternatively, for many of the exercises you could substitute a small whiteboard. You will need marker pens. Scraps of different kinds of paper, old magazines and PVA glue would be useful for some of the exercises which involve collage work. It is useful to keep a folder of the work that you do as you go through the sessions so that you can look back through them. Alternatively you may like to keep a record of your work using digital photographs.

Exercises have 'suggested times' on them. These are not intended to limit you, but are guidelines. If you are working alone, the temptation can be to skip over an exercise too quickly and not get the full benefit of learning from the activity. When you are using this book, make time to do the exercises thoroughly. Each session contains between two and three hours of practical exercises as well as your reading time. You may like to set aside a regular time to work, ideally in a quiet space where you can be sure of not being interrupted.

Because this programme is designed in such a way as to be useable by someone working alone, some of the exercises make use of audio or visual materials from radio or television as a basis for listening exercises. To do these, you will need to be able to replay the recording and to stop it at various points. This can be achieved either by taping the piece which you plan to use, or using the 'listen again' facility on media websites. The latter is probably easiest as it allows you to find suitable material relatively easily and to replay and stop the transmission as required.

SUPPORT

Developing our capacity to engage with others is an exciting journey of discovery. Through listening to the stories of people's lives and the multitude of feeling reactions which they experience, we are ourselves touched and changed. The courage and spirit which people demonstrate in terrible circumstances can be uplifting and humbling for the listener. The despair and hopelessness which others feel can be equally affecting. Also, in hearing of other people's experiences, we are likely to be reminded of our personal stories. Sometimes this can be distressing. Unless we learn ways of sharing these feeling responses, we may find ourselves thrown by the emotional impact of the work we are doing.

In order to do the work, we need to learn to face emotional reactions, both in ourselves and others. People generally want to talk things over with someone else because, for one reason or another, they feel out of their depth or isolated in their situation. Often they feel overwhelmed and part of them wants to escape from the feelings. We cannot really give support to others unless we are able to face difficulties without mentally running away.

Also, at a simple level, we need a familiarity with emotional material and a language for talking about it. Facing our own experiences is important in developing our capacity to under-stand others and not impose our views, but it can be difficult. If, as you read this book and undertake the exercises in it, you find yourself reacting with strong emotions, you may, yourself, feel the need of someone to talk to. This is quite normal. Trainee counsellors are generally expected to spend time with a counsellor themselves, to experience being on the receiving end of the method, but also to explore their personal experiences and reactions.

7

If you find things being stirred up for you, which you feel you do not want to handle on your own, do not be afraid to seek out support. In many helping roles you will have a supervisor. It may be that you can talk to this person about your feelings. If not, you will probably be able to find a counsellor in your locality. Ask around, or look in your telephone directory. Finding the right person to talk to is important and we will discuss this further in session five. Above all though, do not think that you have to carry your feelings alone. This book is about listening, and we need to allow others to listen to us, as well as listening to them.

KEEPING A LEARNING JOURNAL

Thinking about your learning process as you go along will improve your capacity to get more from the exercises. Whilst you are using this book, you may wish to keep a learning journal. This, in itself, can be a useful way of focusing your study. There are many ways of keeping a learning journal, but in particular you may like to:

- Record the exercises you have done (perhaps with photos of drawings).
- Write about your process in doing the exercises. Record what you learned.
- Write about incidents which happen in your working or leisure contexts, where you observe yourself using listening skills.
- Write about incidents which happen in your working or leisure contexts, where you observe instances of things discussed in the book.
- Write about other reading you do, or about material from TV, radio, lectures or workshops which has relevance.
- Read back over earlier entries and annotate them in the light of your later learning.

Since a learning journal can be interactive, keeping it in a computer file may be a creative way of working, as it allows you to go back and add to earlier entries, as well as including photographs. If you do this, feel free to add fresh comments, but do not censor your first reflections. It is useful to look back and see how your thinking has progressed.

Another option you might consider is to keep your journal on-line. For this you would need a password protected site. If you do this, you can even make your reflections available to an on-line peer group. Be aware of issues of confidentiality, however, and do not name or give away clues to the identities of people or organisations you are discussing. In any journal which you keep, think about who might have access to the material and be respectful in your comments.

THE STRUCTURE OF THE BOOK

This book is divided into twelve sections or sessions. These sessions take you through a programme of skills development in a sequence which builds from initial concepts to more sophisticated ideas and methods. These sessions could thus be used as the basis for a group programme.

If this is the case, each session should take at least two to three hours and students would still need to do some exercises and reading in their own time between meetings. Having copies of the book will enable them to revisit themes and re-read theoretical materials. On the other hand, if time allows, there is sufficient material in each session for you to devote far longer to it. Having more time will allow you to do justice to the subject matter.

Working on your own, of course, you have more flexibility. Nevertheless, the book is intended to work as a whole, so it may be most fruitful to aim to complete each session within, say, one or two weeks, so that you reach the end without having lost track of the beginning. If you do this, you can re-visit the early sessions and learn from them at a new level as your experience increases.

TERMINOLOGY

This book is intended for anyone who listens. There are many roles and professions in which developing skill in listening is important, so the appeal of what is contained in this book is broad. The material in the book is presented in a way that starts with an assumption of no prior knowledge or experience. You simply need to be willing to engage with the process. At the same time, the book offers a perspective on the listening process which may be of interest to counsellors and therapists who already have a solid base of skills. It is practical in its orientation and offers a solid grounding for social workers, community workers, chaplains, nurses or other professionals whose business is caring.

Each of these professions has its own particular settings and preferred terminology. For this reason it is hard to identify one term which will fit all readers. For simplicity's sake, I have decided, in general, to use the term 'listener' to describe the person engaged in listening, counselling, pastoral care, or whatever other occupation the reader is engaged in.

The same dilemmas apply when discussing the settings and the recipients of this kind of focused-listening. Again, for simplicity's sake, I need to adopt a generic term. I will therefore, in most cases, refer to the person being listened to as the 'service user', though occasionally the word 'client' (as used in the counselling and social work professions) may be more appropriate. In referring to the context where listening takes place, I will generally use the words 'agency' or 'setting'. I hope the reader will bear with this and appreciate my dilemma in the matter.

FURTHER STUDY

This book includes information about its main theoretical sources in the end notes. If you wish to take your studies further you will find suggestions there for future reading.

Session One

Wanting to listen

This session will explore:

- The listening context
- Personal paths to listening work
- Hopes and fears involved in developing listening skills
- Studying in groups or alone

This book is for anyone who wants to listen better. It is for anyone who hears other people talking about ways in which they are troubled but feels inadequate when it is their turn to give a response. In this, it is a book which could be helpful to anyone. We all interact with other people and the quality of that inter-action makes a lot of difference to our lives.

Mostly though, this book is intended for the many people who listen to others in the many different contexts that we could broadly think of as helping situations, whether these are in voluntary or professional settings. It provides a starting point for volunteer listeners and counsellors, nurses, chaplains, social workers and advice workers, teachers and support workers, and all the other people engaged in regular one-to-one dialogue with people who are facing troubles.

With such a broad group in mind, you will need to use this book intelligently. This is always going to be the case with a book of inter-personal skills, for each person you meet will be different, with different needs. However, some differences are contextual, and as we go through the different concepts and exercises included here, you will find that some are more helpful and relevant to your situation than others.

Some of the exercises in this book are included because they directly relate to things you might do and say in a listening context, but others are for your own benefit, helping you to think more deeply about your own life experience. As you experiment and try things out, think about whether they might be useful or adaptable to the context you are working in, but mostly, do them for yourself and see what they have to teach you.

If you are reading this book, it is likely that you already have in mind some context in which you will put the skills that you learn into practice. You may already be in a role where listening is important, and be looking at ways of developing your skills. On the other hand, you may be starting out, looking for a new direction and for guidance in how to embark on a new path. Whether or not you have a specific setting in mind, this book will guide you in both looking at what experience you already have to offer, and in looking at where that experience might be applied.

The history which we bring to the listening role is an important factor. It not only affects what we choose to do, but also the way in which we respond to other people. Our history creates the conditions within which we operate. It shapes our attitudes and our way of speaking. It also shapes our understanding and even what we notice about the other person. Thus our past can be a very positive influence on what we do. It can give us sensitivity and make us more aware of others' needs, but it can also narrow our expectations and lead us into making assumptions. It is good to be aware of such potential pitfalls.

Throughout this book we will return again and again to this theme of the interaction between our own lives and our developing skill as listeners. It is important that we are aware of just how conditioned our view is, of the heritage of information and intuition which we carry, but also of the dangers and limitations that our history imposes. We are always at risk of assuming that how we see the world is 'how it is'.

On the other hand, if we become more aware of our roots, the knowledge and skills which we have acquired over the years will become a resource which we can tap into. Most of us are far more

.sensitive to our surroundings, and to the nuances of speech and gesture, than we realise. Social censorship and propriety have discouraged us from expressing the intuitions and resonances which arise in everyday conversation. In intentional listening, it is often on this hidden awareness which we learn to draw.

This first session will, therefore, focus on exploring your own route to this vocation. What is it that has led you to want to offer yourself as someone who listens to others? What resources do you have, and what barriers might your past create?

Personal Paths

What is it that leads us to want to offer support to others? For different people there will be different answers. Usually our motivations are complex. Sometimes specific events have led us into the work. These might include a distressing experience of our own, such as a bereavement, illness or childhood trauma. It might be that we have a concern for a particular group of people, perhaps because we have a relative or friend with a special need. We might be inspired by our beliefs, whether social, religious or political. We might have realised that we enjoy talking in depth with people, that others find us supportive, or that we have an aptitude for the work. We might have specialist knowledge to offer in a specific advice work context. We might have time on our hands and be looking for ways of giving something back to society, or we might have stumbled into the work by accident because our career path took us there. All these possibilities (and there are many more) contribute to our sense of what we can offer. They may determine the particular context in which we work. They affect our confidence and our attitudes in approaching the role of listener.

Our involvement in listening work usually has a history. Even when one incident has been the trigger for volunteering or for a change of career, a person who seeks this kind of occupation has probably already experienced a number of things which have pointed him or her in this direction, and has perhaps since childhood, had experiences which have contributed to the process of learning to be sensitive to others.

EXERCISE ONE: LIFE-LINE EXERCISE

(about twenty minutes)

On a sheet of paper, draw a diagram of your route to wanting to develop your listening skills. Start from birth and draw a time-line from left to right across your page.

On the line mark significant events or phases in your life. For each one mark down what you learned that might be relevant to becoming a listener.

My Route to This Course

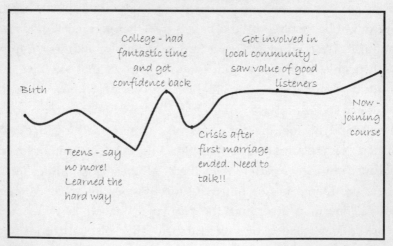

Reflect back over the diagram and list some of the key incidents on another sheet of paper or in your journal. For

---

each incident, jot down what you learned that may be helpful to you in becoming a listener, and also what pitfalls might arise from that experience.

Exploring our personal paths to becoming a listener can be helpful for two reasons.

Firstly, the exploration makes us more aware of the way that our thinking is coloured. We might refer to this by saying that our view is *conditioned*. We become more aware of factors which may be in the background of our thinking about the work.

Conditioned view can lead us to expect others to react the way that we did in similar circumstances. It can make us intolerant of third parties involved, or with people who understand the situation differently. Once we become aware of these limits, we can make allowances for them and try to get beyond them and incorporate other perspectives into our thinking. Indeed, as we make the effort to get beyond our assumptions and hear what is really being said, we will naturally develop a more complex, rounded, view.

Secondly, however, reflecting on our personal path can help us to draw on the vast resources which our experiences have given us. Our own history can be helpful in enabling us to understand others' situations, and help us to feel sympathetic to those who suffer similar difficulties to our own. Even when the actual circumstances of a person's life are very different, the fact that we are aware of our own grief, frustration, anger or disappointment can help us understand something of how the other person might be feeling and why their particular situation feels so distressing to them. For example, reflecting on the disappointment you felt at failing an exam might give insight into some aspects of how another person might feel whose career has just been brought to an end by compulsory redundancy. By thinking about the way that things have unfolded in our own case, we develop a better understanding of the impact of circumstances on other people and the complexity of reactions a person may have. When we realise the mistakes and misfortunes we have experienced over the years, this can give us humility and remind us that in many situations there are no simple solutions and people make mistakes with the best of intentions.

When we reflect on good things which have happened or ways in which we have been supported or loved by others, this can put us in touch with the things which inspired us in the past and with the current sources of inspiration in our lives.

Inspiration and Influences

In exercise one you looked at incidents and life experiences which have influenced your path to becoming a listener. Your exploration may well have led you to think of particular people who have been influential in your choice to take up this kind of work. Most of us can think of people whom we look up to. These might be people whom we have known personally or public figures. They might be people whom we have actually met, or people we have read about or seen on film. They might inspire us because of their life story, or for particular things they did. Even people whose lives are quite ordinary in other ways may have inspired us because they did or said something out of the ordinary on a particular occasion. Often we are inspired by people without realising it. Sometimes, for example, a relative or even an ancestor has had more influence than we imagined, and it is only when we start to reflect on their life that we realise our own life has followed a similar course.

EXERCISE TWO: NET DIAGRAM EXERCISE
(ten minutes)

Look at the diagram you created in exercise one. Are there people who were particularly influential at different points in your life? Maybe there were particular people whom you associate with the incidents which you recalled. Make a list of people who have been important to you.

Now think about other figures who have been a source of inspiration to you. These might be people you have known, but you can include other people who you know of but have never met, for example, from the news or from history.

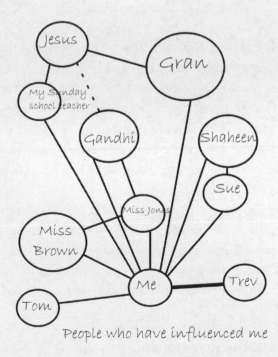

People who have influenced me

Draw a diagram showing all of these people and linking them to the point that represents you. If appropriate, you can link them to each other too, to show lines of influence. For example, you might do this to show that you and a friend were both influenced by a political or religious leader.

If you want to develop this diagram, you can add in a second level of other people who were inspirational to the people who inspired you, for example, who was it that inspired your favourite teacher at school? Did they have an indirect influence on you? Beside each person you can write a few words which describe what you received from them. Write some notes about your discoveries.

When we think of the people who have been important to us over the years, we may feel gratitude for their influence, or appreciation for their human spirit. Sometimes, looking back, we come to view them in new ways, seeing new aspects to how they were. Holding people in respect and appreciation is an important aspect of our personal journey. We do not achieve things alone and all of us owe much to the many people who have helped us to learn and develop.

The habit of appreciation is one that is important in the support process. If we are appreciative of those who have helped us in the past, we will also develop our capacity to appreciate those whom we encounter in our present work. As we appreciate them, they in turn will grow more appreciative of life and become happier.

There are other sources of inspiration too. We may have been inspired by ideas or by art, by natural beauty or by the processes of life. We may be inspired by political theory or by social movements, by the spiritual dimension of life or by our religious faith. Such inspiration is an important foundation for our work. Our sense of meaning and purpose is the well from which we draw our capacity to give to others. For some people, this source will be already clearly articulated in social, spiritual or religious ideas, but for others it may be a more generalised confidence in the life process.

EXERCISE THREE: EXPLORING INSPIRATION MEDITATION
(twenty minutes)

Find a quiet space in which to sit. Place a large sheet of paper and some coloured chalks or pens in front of you. Close your eyes and breathe slowly and consciously for a few minutes, then ask yourself:

What is it that underpins my life?

This is an invitation to explore the values, beliefs and inspiration which lie at the base of your experience. Different people will have different language for expressing this. You may think in religious terms, but equally you may think about attitudes or guiding principles. You may think things like 'people are basically trustworthy' or 'the universe is infinitely mysterious' or 'live for the moment', or you may think of God or Buddha.

On your sheet of paper, write down whatever words or phrases seem to speak to you, or draw images which express your sense of what holds and inspires you. Write as many words as you can, drawing out different qualities

---

and attributes which connect with your source of inspiration. Make your page colourful and joyous.

Put your page in a place where you can see it through the week, and reflect from time to time on whether you wish to add to it or change anything.

How far do you feel you will be able to draw on this resource in your work? Are there ways in which you can develop your connection with it so that it becomes stronger?

Hopes and Anxieties

Learning any new skill can be emotionally taxing. As a beginner, it can be exciting to see a whole new world of possibilities opening up before us and realise that there are things we can learn of which we had no idea. At the same time, it can feel uncomfortable to attempt to do something in a new way and realise that one has to re-learn a whole lot of things that one has been doing for years. As with learning any new skill, when you start to become a listener, you can feel very 'wooden' and inhibited. It can be a struggle to master new ways of interacting, and self-consciousness can make us clumsy.

If you are learning in a group there may be extra fears. You may feel anxious about looking silly in front of others, or be worried that you may not be able to handle things that others reveal about themselves. Even if you are studying on your own, at some point you will want to use your listening skills in interacting with others and then you may feel anxious about being observed by third parties. This can be particularly the case for someone already established in a professional role. There can be a pressure

20

to appear competent even when one doesn't feel it.

At this point, then, let us look at what anxieties you might be bringing to the role of listener, to studying with this book, and to the process of learning. Let us also explore what hopes you have of the experience.

EXERCISE FOUR: HOPES AND FEARS
(about twenty-five minutes)

Take a sheet of paper and divide it into six boxes as follows:

Exploring My Hopes and Fears

Hopes for working on this course	Hopes for working in this group / for working on the material on my own	Hopes about using the things I have learned
Fears for working on this course	Hopes for working in this group / for working on the material on my own	Hopes about using the things I have learned

Use the grid to write down whatever hopes and fears come to mind in relation to this study programme itself, to the study situation (whether in a group or on your own) and to applying what you learn in a listening context.

When you have finished, look at each thing you have written and mark it 'Realistic', 'Unrealistic' or 'Not Sure'.

> Of course, 'realistic' might mean two things; it might mean that your fear or hope is understandable or it might mean that there is something in the situation that you need to be wary of.
>
> Reflect on what you have written and discuss it in your journal or with a learning partner.

Human interactions are unpredictable and it is in the nature of helping situations that sometimes we may encounter people who are in extreme situations or states of mind. In such positions it is easy to feel out of one's depth. Sometimes the listener feels that they should be able to "fix" what is wrong. Although rationally we know this is impossible, we still buy into ideas that we should have the capacity to sort anything out. It is not surprising therefore that many people feel anxious about the responsibility which will be involved in listening to others, and that sometimes people are frightened of particular situations arising.

Looking honestly at our anxieties is helpful. In some cases we may come to feel that our worries are well founded. It is appropriate to assess our limits and to think about how we might cope if things went wrong. Other anxieties diminish when we look at them. Things are not as bad as we thought. Many anxieties simply reflect inexperience. We can acknowledge them, but then proceed, trusting that, as we gain confidence, they will subside. In all this, the guidance of someone with more experience can be very valuable. Talking through anxieties with a supervisor or mentor helps to put them in perspective.

Having looked at our anxieties and treated them seriously, however, it is also important to give space to our hopes and our faith in what we are doing. Our positive intuitions about the learning process and the work we will be undertaking are the source of energy from which our capacity to help will grow. If we are undertaking this sort of work, it is probably because we have confidence that it is worthwhile and healing. We have faith in the value of personal connection with others. We are inspired by the possibilities for change and growth which listening offers. We treasure the unique possibilities in each interaction.

Learning Alone or as a Group

You may be reading this book on your own, but maybe you are studying in a group. For the benefit of those studying in a group, this section will look at group learning and, particularly, at some of the things which may arise at the start of groups. Whilst it is not in the scope of this book to look at groupwork theory in detail, it is useful to offer some guidance for groups who do wish to use this material in this way. In this session I will therefore particularly consider some of the issues involved in establishing group space.

Even if you are not currently working in a group, it is likely that you will be involved with groups from time to time. If you are interested in interpersonal work, you will invariably find yourself enjoying some group learning experiences. You may even choose to set up groups for people you are supporting. You may, therefore, still like to reflect on the material in this section.

GROUND RULES
One of the first things that groups do is to establish their mode of operating. Whether or not a group formally agrees on a set of rules or guidelines, every group settles into particular customary ways of treating one another. A lot of the early stages of a group are taken up in direct or indirect negotiation of these matters. Sometimes it is useful to make this aspect of the process explicit.

For this reason, it is common practice in some types of group to start off by talking about what expectations members have of one another in terms of behaviour. This is a good way for group members to get to know one another and find out what common ground they have. It can also help prevent misunderstandings, but it will not eliminate these entirely. Even when a group has agreed to ground rules, members may well break the rules later and new norms may develop as the group goes on. This is a normal part of group behaviour and shows that the group is alive and growing.

EXERCISE FIVE: EXPECTATIONS AND GROUND RULES

(fifteen minutes: note that groups may like to tackle this exercise early in the first session)

If you are in a group:
Discuss the following in pairs:
- What sort of things are you expecting from this group?
- Are there things that you would like other people to do?
- Are there things that you don't want?
- What are your hopes and fears?

Write your responses on a flip chart and share with the group. Based on these responses, your group may wish to go on to agree some basic ground rules.

If you are working on your own:
Reflect on your experiences of groups which you have participated in. What sort of atmosphere was there in the group? What sort of ground rules (explicitly agreed or implicit from the group's behaviour) were in place? Did these change as the group continued?

In practice, most ground rules boil down to respecting one another.

CONFIDENTIALITY

In particular, you may want to think about the issue of confidentiality. What sorts of things are you happy for group members to share outside the group, and what should be kept within the group? Confidentiality is something which often concerns people, especially when they do not yet know or trust each other, or know what the group may involve.

Discussing what you understand by confidentiality can help your group to get to know each other better, as well as helping you to align on expectations. At the same time, you will probably not reach a final view on this matter until you have experienced working together as a group. Whatever you agree, be prepared to discuss matters further as the reality of group life unfolds.

STONE PASSING

In the Amida community, where I live, we use stone passing as a way of listening to one another. This method is based on one used by many groups. For example, many people will have heard of the Native American practice of using a talking stick. Stone passing is similar. It is a good way for groups to share. You may like to use it in order to create space for people to talk. The way that we use stone passing can vary, but most commonly we use the following rules.

After a few minutes silence, someone in the group will be given the stone. That person then shares whatever she or he wishes, talking personally, from the heart (rather than theorising). When she or he has finished, the stone is passed to another member of the group. The second person can share whatever he or she wishes, not necessarily responding to the first person. The stone is passed in this way to everyone in the group. After everyone has had a turn, it is placed in the centre of the group on the floor. Now anyone can pick up the stone and add to what has already been said.

You can say whatever you like when you have the stone and do not need to follow on from the previous person. If someone asks you a question, you do not have to answer. If you do want to answer, you must wait until you get the stone. If you do not want to speak, you may say so and pass the stone on, but you will then have to wait until the stone is put in the middle before you get a turn. The gathering ends when everyone has finished and the group falls into silence or when an agreed time is up.

A stone passing creates a good environment for sharing because it offers a balance of formality and space. The practice of passing the stone introduces an element of ritual and this has the effect of:

- Increasing seriousness.
- Getting people to listen with good attention. You can't interrupt, so you do not need to be planning what to say next. You can concentrate on the person who is speaking.
- Giving time to talk that is set apart with time boundaries.
- Giving a form, so everyone knows what is expected.
- Giving freedom to say what you want to. The rules say that you don't have to respond in particular ways, so you can change the subject or not respond to other people's questions unless you want to.

LEARNING ON YOUR OWN

Whilst some people will develop their skills through learning in a group, this book is also intended for the person who wants to learn more about listening skills working on their own. This aspect of the material is perhaps particularly valuable, since many agencies run listening skills courses, but there are fewer resources for the person who, for one reason or another, cannot tap into such training. In particular, the practical nature of the book, with its focus on exercises rather than theory, should provide a means to develop your skills in a realistic way. To do this, however, requires your co-operation and ingenuity.

CREATING YOUR OWN LEARNING SPACE

The exercises in this book will help you to explore aspects of the subject. They offer structures, but you will need to create space in which you can discover personal meaning in them. This means devoting time which is focused, and as far as possible uninterrupted, to doing the exercises.

The learning environment you choose is important in facilitating this process. In order to do an exercise properly you need to create a quiet space. It is unlikely you could do an exercise effectively in a crowded room or on a moving train. It is therefore good to set aside a space in your house where you can study and reflect. If we use such a place regularly, it becomes a base, which gets associated in our minds with reflection, and, thus, conditions good quality learning. So think about the space where you will go to read and practise the exercises contained in this book.

Space is also temporal. Making time for the work is important, and this is perhaps one of the biggest difficulties for the person studying alone. Whereas the group member is, de facto, carried along by the group timetable, it is easy for lone study time to be eroded by impinging duties (especially as those who want to offer listening are often busy people who, because they care, are continually offering to take on extra work for others!)

Learning is about dialogue. This may be dialogue with people, or with written materials or tasks. The human aspect of this is generally important and working on your own, you may feel a lack of stimulation. The book itself will offer some contribution to a dialectic process. You can argue with what is written, reflect on it, write responses to it, but unfortunately, unless you contact me directly, it will not answer back. You may feel the need for more response.

There are various ways to increase your sense of dialogue with the material. You may engage in active dialogue with yourself. Read back over old notes, and keep a learning journal. Reflect on what you have written, or explore by using different 'voices'. Do also, though, find opportunities to discuss what you are learning with others who have an interest in the field. Find a mentor or supervisor and peers you can discuss matters with. Join an on-line peer support group, as suggested in the introduction.

EXERCISE SIX: HOW DO I LEARN?
(five minutes)

Think about your own pattern of learning. What sort of things do you find helpful to the process of studying? What sort of environments do you choose for work that requires concentration? Does the space you choose vary according to the task you are doing?

Reflect on the study which will be involved in following this book. Is it like other learning you have done, or are there new challenges? How can you make it effective and meaningful for yourself?

What sort of needs do you have in relation to this study? Think about the following dimensions of the learning process and how you might support them:
• Focused time for reading and reflection
• Opportunities for dialogue with other students or practitioners
• Opportunities to practise skills
• Meditative space to develop grounding and concentration
• Creative time to develop your imaginative powers
• Personal support to talk about emotions

Session Two

Contexts and Conditions

This session will include:

- Settings and situations
- Conditioned views and expectations
- The use of structure and space in listening situations
- Sacred space, the listening environment and learning process

As we saw in the last session, our experience and history are important factors in conditioning what we are able to offer to others. When we listen to others, our listening is always grounded in our own mentality. Although we are mostly unaware of it, our past, beliefs, attitudes and habits shape what we hear and what we say. Becoming more aware of the distortion which we bring to the listening process, as well as of the strengths these personal aspects contribute, helps us to connect better with others, and to realise what may be going wrong when we find ourselves missing the point of what they are saying.

The context in which the listening takes place, however, also brings its own set of conditions. There may be ways of thinking that are part of the culture of that organisation or agency. These may have developed out of the particular circumstances or client group which the agency serves and be reflected in activities which go on there, in the language which people in the agency use, and in their habits of thought and behaviour. These cultural phenomena impinge on us and create a background to our work. We are affected by them and may be infected by the attitudes and behaviours they give rise to.

Within this agency context, people bring their own individual stories and their individual ways of being. Despite the collective ethos, individually they may embody quite different sets of cultural norms, ideas and assumptions. It is as if each person exists in a bubble of their own story, habits and mental phenomena, but that this bubble is permeable to a greater or lesser degree, allowing the context to add colouration and biases.

In listening to others, we create a dialogue between three worlds. We bring together the world of our own experiences and that of the people we are working with and that of the context of our meeting. Such dialogue has the potential to be very exciting and fulfilling.

Settings

Supportive listening takes place in many settings. These each impose different conditions on the listener and on the person using the agency. They have an effect on what is possible. The setting is one factor that creates conditions for the process of listening. Without listing again the plethora of settings in which listening happens, let us look at some of the different types of feature that different contexts might offer. In reading these you may like to bear in mind both the setting in which you are currently operating and other settings with which you are familiar.

THE PURPOSE OF THE AGENCY

Different contexts will impose their own limits on the listening relationship. The agency purpose is an obvious example of this. If the agency is concerned with debt counselling, the listener will have very little remit to explore, for example, the user's grief over a partner's death, except in as much as it is impacting on the family finances. Conversely, an agency concerned with grief counselling may well offer the person who needs financial advice a referral for specialist help.

The problem with such demarcations is, of course, that people's lives are not necessarily so neatly compartmentalised.

The grieving widow may not gain the strength to make tough financial decisions until her grief has diminished, and her misery may be exacerbated by her stricken circumstances.

Nevertheless, we all operate within certain limits, and a good network of contacts to whom one can refer people will help to reduce the possible harm done by some of these limitations.

THE ROLE OF THE LISTENER WITHIN THE AGENCY

Some agencies, by their nature, impose a limit on the listener, but others are complex organisations within which different workers may have different roles. This will create limits on what a particular worker can do within the organisation as a whole. For example, within a hospital, there may be a number of people who all use listening skills, but each of these workers has an area of expertise. The nurse, the volunteer, the hospital visitor, the social worker, the chaplain, the counsellor, the surgeon, the dietician, the auxiliary staff, as well as other specialist advisors, may all, at times, be involved in using listening skills. Sometimes their role will be completely focused around counselling, other times listening will be an activity which supports their main function. Each will bring a particular style of working and a designated agenda.

Here, team work becomes important, though this is not without its problems. Clients may not wish to be passed between team members for different aspects of their care and may want to continue to confide in the person whom they have chosen to trust. There may also be issues of confidentiality, as discussions between colleagues can become rather casual.

THE CLIENT GROUP BEING SERVED

Depending on their purpose, many agencies will have a client group which they are established to serve. This may be defined by any number of factors such as age, life situation, disease, disability, gender, race, or faith. Some client groups have particular needs and capacities which will affect the listening process. A teenager may need a less formal setting; a person with hearing impairment may need assistance with signing or a place that is private enough so that louder conversation will not be overheard. An asylum seeker may need translation, or a woman may need to talk to another woman.

Besides these special needs, different client groups will bring their own cultural norms and their own special qualities to the setting. Some cultures may be very sociable and family orientated, for example, and a listener working in such groups might need to take into account differences of expectation around confidentiality and privacy. I recall working with one group on an estate in the north of England. When I suggested we discuss confidentiality, the group just burst out laughing. They anticipated that whatever was shared in the meeting would be the hot topic in their street all the following week. My suggestion that things might be confidential seemed like middleclass claptrap.

This incident challenged my assumptions and taught me how flexible groups could be. The lack of agreement did not prevent us having a lively discussion with plenty of personal sharing. Sometimes the lack of privacy in such a group could be a problem, but in that instance, the sociable culture meant that users of the group were able to tap into extensive family or community support networks.

So different cultures bring richness, as well as problems, to the group process, and in order to appreciate this, the listener may tune into cultural as well as individual qualities in the service users, to find out what is possible, and to identify how this particular group handles the different interpersonal problems which groups encounter.

EXERCISE ONE: EXPLORING AGENCY FACTORS

(fifteen minutes)

Think about the agency in which you are, or intend to offer your services as a listener. Write a brief profile of the agency.

- What is the purpose of the agency you are involved in, or the role which you have within the agency?
- Within that purpose, what subjects might be appropriate to discuss in a listening session, and what might be outside the agency remit?
- What might happen if a person wants to discuss something outside the remit which you have identified? Is there a process of referral?
- What client group or groups is the agency set up to work with?
- How far does this client group create particular needs?
- How are these reflected in the style of listening offered?
- What resources, if any, might the client group, as a whole, offer to an individual who was in difficulties?
- Do you see obvious gaps which you might want to investigate or rectify?

Make notes of your responses and refer back to them. If you are not yet involved in an agency, you may like to return to this exercise at a later date.

The client group and purpose for which the agency is established define certain parameters for the listening process. These parameters may be translated into ways of operating. Ways of operating work well when they are suitable for the context in which they are being employed. Some ways of operating, however, can be imposed for other reasons, which may or may not benefit the users. Other reasons might include:

- The orientation or therapeutic model of the agency
- Practicalities relating to buildings or equipment
- Practicalities relating to safety, security and good practice procedures
- Protecting the agency from complaint and litigation
- Worker preference and convenience
- History and habit
- Things which went wrong in the past

As you can see, some of these factors are based on important considerations and need to be taken into account, but others are simply about convenience or personal preference and may not necessarily create the best working situation or a more supportive environment.

Other factors, which affect the listening process, arise from the style of service which is offered:

ACCESS TO THE SERVICE

The service may be limited to a particular group of people. Access may also be restricted in a variety of other ways; for example, by means testing, benefit rules and other financial restrictions, physical location and accessibility of buildings, timing of sessions, language and culture. Some restrictions will be absolute and are intentionally imposed because of the nature of the agency, whilst others operate more as practical or psychological barriers experienced by certain users. For example, a woman may feel uncomfortable using a service where all the workers are men. It is always good practice for an agency to look at issues of access and to decide whether some potential users are being inappropriately excluded by problems of accessibility.

LEVELS OF PRIVACY

People often feel safer talking in a room where they will not be seen or interrupted. Even something like an opaque glass door can be off-putting. Being able to hear other people talking outside the door can lead the person who is talking to fear that they may, in turn, be overheard. On the other hand, some people may feel safer talking if other people are around in the background, and may find going off into a private room too intense or threatening. For them, the informal atmosphere of a drop-in or coffee morning may feel less daunting.

Different settings offer and require different levels of privacy. In a drop-in session, listeners may sit at tables and chat to users, or play cards or snooker. A crisis counselling service will probably use closed consultation rooms where the user cannot be overheard. Sometimes the level of privacy can be varied according to need. The listener at the drop-in might sense a person's need to talk more seriously and invite them into a side room or take them for a walk, for example.

Judging the best setting for talking is something that comes with experience. Someone who is very timid may feel more comfortable with other people around. Someone who is crying may not want others to see. Do not be afraid to ask the person if they would prefer to go somewhere quiet. Sometimes, however, you may just need to make the decision for the person, especially if they are very distressed.

Occasionally there may be safety concerns about going into a room on your own with someone, for example, if they are very disturbed or have a history of violence. If this is the case, trust your intuition and do not take the risk. Whether or not you are right, you will not be very supportive as a listener if you are frightened. It is better to stay in a public space and listen in a more relaxed way.

Usually, if the situation is clear to service users, they will make their own decisions about what to talk about. Problems tend to arise if the person assumes there is more privacy than there actually is. The listener may need to protect the person who is talking from being inadvertently overheard either because they are too distressed, or because they lack the social ability to notice the other people who are around, or because a room is not as sound proof as it appears to be. Issues of privacy also extend to any record keeping. This issue will be discussed later.

TIME LIMITS

Some listening sessions are time-limited, whilst others can theoretically go on for as long as is required. Some are arranged in advance, and may occur regularly for a given length of time. Others are spontaneous meetings, happening when a need arises. Such differences can arise for any of the reasons already discussed. They will affect what is possible. Once again, from the user's point of view, what is required is clarity about what is on offer. Differences of expectation that are not clarified cause problems and lead to bad feelings.

IS THE MEETING FOCUSED ON AN ISSUE, AND HOW IMPORTANT IS IT?

Not all listening situations involve someone coming to talk about a problem. In situations like hospital visiting or a community project, the initial contact between listener and user may be casual and social. Only occasionally may more serious matters emerge. Here the listener needs to gauge the nature of the conversation and adapt the tone of response accordingly.

When an issue is presented, the degree of seriousness with which it is voiced and its importance to the client or user are likely to affect the ensuing interaction and its outcome. If the client does not see the problem as significant, things are unlikely to change, even if professionals dealing with the matter are concerned.

EXERCISE TWO: DIFFERENT AGENCIES, DIFFERENT STYLES
(ten minutes)

Think of two agencies with which you are familiar, which operate in different ways. They do not need to be places you have worked in or intend to work in. In fact, it may be useful to look at places where you have been a user. Take a large sheet of paper and divide it into two vertical columns. Write the names of one agency on the top of the first column, and the other on the second.

Use the columns to explore contrasting features of the ways that each of the agencies operates, listing the characteristics of each in the labelled column. Include in your comments broad observations about purpose and user groups, and narrower details about the actual style of service offered.

Reflect on why each agency does things the way that they do. How much is style driven by the purpose and needs, and how far is it affected by other factors? What differences do you notice in the effects of different styles of operation? Which environment is conducive to what sort of atmosphere?

Conditions and Expectations

The setting in which you operate as a listener will affect the work that you do in all manner of ways. As we have already seen, there are big differences in the scope and style of listening that can be offered. Many of these differences are not based on the choice of the listener, but are established by the agency, so you may want to bear these in mind when you initially choose to work in a particular area.

You will probably want to find a place to work which fits with your sense of what you can offer. There will be practical aspects to this. You are likely to look for a setting which is right for your level of experience and aptitude. If you are a counsellor, advice work may be limiting and frustrating. If you are new to the work, you may feel out of your depth with people with severe mental health problems.

Something which may be harder to judge, and more significant, is the general ethos of the agency. It is often more important to feel that you are on the same wave length as the people you are working with (both other listeners and users) than to feel an exact alignment on a job description.

EXPECTATIONS

Having looked at some of the conditions which impact upon the listening relationship and which are connected with the agency in which the listening is happening, let us now go on to look at some of the conditions which operate from our own side as listeners.

When we first encounter a person whom we have not met before, we bring with us a set of expectations. As we have discussed, these expectations colour what we see and also shape what we expect will happen. We have these expectations because our minds are *conditioned*. Conditioning happens in a number of ways, but common ones include:

- History: things that we have done or thought before; past experiences of talking to people or experiences of learning.
- Circumstances: the current situation we are in; the setting in which the meeting is happening; the décor and layout of the room; our associations with 'getting advice', 'groups' or 'other people'.
- What happened last: what we were doing before we came into

the room or as we walked through the door?

- What is in front of us: the thing that is catching our attention at that time.
- Our sense of who we are and our habitual responses.

In the last session we looked at expectations which you had at the start of this book. Look back at the expectations which you identified in Session One, Exercise Three. Think about what might have caused you to think of them at the point in time when you did the exercise. What conditioned your mind so that you thought of those particular hopes and fears, rather than other ones you might have thought of at another time? If you were repeating the exercise today, would a different set of expectations occur to you? Why?

EXERCISE THREE: EXPLORING CONTEXT AND REACTIONS

(about fifteen to twenty minutes)

Take a big sheet of paper and draw a circle in the centre of it, about the size of a dinner plate. In the circle write a word or short phrase that describes the context in which you are already offering listening, or might offer it in the future (this might be something like 'volunteer project' or 'church'). Use bold letters so that these words will be clear when you look at the page from a distance. (If you are working in several contexts choose one scenario to work with.)

When you have done this, fill the rest of the circle with words which describe that context. These might be things you notice or expect to notice there, words that describe the service users or the place, or things about the general

---

atmosphere. Include anything you associate with the situation, the people or the place. Write freely, allowing yourself to imaginatively be there 'in the situation'. If some of the things that occur to you seem odd, do not censor them, just write them down. You can think about what they might mean later. *(Take about five minutes over this first part of the exercise.)*

Now read what you have written. Try not to become analytical or self-critical. Just read what is there. Sit and look at the sheet for about five minutes without writing. Shut your eyes and try to really see the situation and feel yourself in it. Imagine approaching a specific person with whom you are going to have a conversation. If you think of more words to describe what you see, add them to the words in the circle.

Now reflect on what you are experiencing as you look at the scenario. Use the space outside the circle to record your reactions. Again, do not censor your thoughts. Just write down whatever comes to you. You can include associations, feelings, thoughts, things which you would like to say, judgements, or anything else which comes into your mind. *(Take a further five minutes to do this.)*

Finally, spend some time looking at your sheet. Do not write anything more. Notice how you feel when you look at it. Are you surprised by any of your observations or reactions? Do you feel embarrassed or critical of yourself? Do you feel anxieties or impulses? What do you learn about the relationship between you and the situation which you are going into? Make some notes in your journal.

CONDITIONED THINKING

What we see is conditioned by our mentality. This is a short way of saying that all our history, attitudes, current circumstances, ways of thinking and so on create the conditions for us to see the world in particular ways. Our viewpoint conditions what we see.

At the same time, the things that we experience affect our mental state. What we see conditions our viewpoint. In other words, there is a circular relationship. We see what we expect to see, based upon what we have seen before, but what we see in turn gives rise to what we go on seeing.

WHAT WE SEE

OUR HISTORY,
ATTITUDES &
VIEWPOINT

Confused? Well, it is confusing, because it is hard to sort out what leads to what. How much do our expectations colour our view, and how much does what we see colour our expectations? To make this practical, which always helps, return to exercise three.

The words in the circle describe what you see. The words outside it describe your response. Reflect on what conditioned what. How objective are the words inside the circle? What do they say about you? Are they emphasising a particular aspect of the situation? Are they the same words a colleague might use? What might somebody who were visiting from another country or culture have written?

Now look at the words outside the circle. How much are these reflecting a mood or a mindset which is conditioned by the particular setting? How much do they reflect your more general attitudes and beliefs?

These themes are ones which we will return to, but at present, it is useful to reflect upon how our initial contact with an agency or client might be coloured by a variety of factors, including expectations, associations, your own history, first impressions and the agency's approach to you.

Creating a Listening Space

STRUCTURE AND SPACE

Any sort of listening relationship happens in a context. In order to offer someone the space to talk, we need to create certain conditions. This book is about learning to offer better conditions for a person who needs some form of support or guidance. It is about learning the flexibility to be able to respond in different ways and different settings so that the other person feels held and respected.

One simple way of conceptualising the listening role is to think in terms of structure and space. Creating a situation in which someone feels comfortable to talk involves these two things:

- We need to offer a structure
- We need to create space

The structure which we offer to the person who has come to speak with us may be something very simple. We might invite them to speak, we might ask a question, we might take them into a private room and shut the door, we might go through a form with them, or we might arrange to meet them on a particular day for an hour. All of these are structures. All involve a sort of invitation for the other person to do something, and all of them provide a starting point.

In some cases, our initial invitation to the person suggests a way of working or a framework within which they can explore their experience. This might be a question or a suggestion of an activity or an exercise. Even suggesting a length of time which the conversation might go on for gives an indication of a sort of framework to the person. So a structure often includes an invitation to talk and a framework for working.

Having offered some sort of structure, we then need to hold back and offer a space. We need to listen. We hold the boundaries of the space by making sure that interruptions are kept to a minimum, but then we clear our minds as far as possible and focus our attention on the other person.

In any listening situation, the element of structure gives the listening its seriousness and increases its intensity. The structure might be as simple as sitting together in a quiet place away from interruptions. The point is that this deliberately creates a situation that is set apart from ordinary social interaction. The person knows that in this context something different is allowed, and even expected.

The sort of structure which we offer will be different for different people. Structure which will be helpful for one person may be unhelpful to someone else. A teenager may feel uncomfortable with too much intensity, for example, and may prefer to talk over the pool table, whereas a woman who is struggling over whether to end her marriage may appreciate the privacy of a side room. Thus, one factor in deciding what to offer will be the amount of intensity which will suit the client or user. Some situations feel more intense than others. What is comfortable for one person may be overpowering for someone else.

Sometimes we may offer more elaborate structures. For example, we might use exercises like the ones in this book, which could help a person to think about what they are saying in a different way, but this is unusual. Mostly listening is about creating conditions in which we can give quality space. Our aim is to give good attention, but not to impose our views. We offer just enough structure to help the person to talk, without imposing our ideas. Generally we avoid doing things which will change the direction of what the person is saying, though we might ask them to go over what they have said again or invite them to look at it in more depth.

EXERCISE FOUR: STRUCTURE AND INVITATION

(ten minutes)

Think about a number of situations when you have talked about personal issues.

What sort of structures were in place that made it feel all right to talk? How much privacy did you have? Were you aware of any time limits? What sort of invitation did you feel you were given that allowed you to talk? (The invitation may not necessarily have been explicit. It may just have been implied by the person's manner.)

Reflect on one of the experiences and imagine how it would have been if the structure had been different. How would it have felt to talk in a more private space or, conversely, a more public space?

Make notes of your observations.

WISDOM AND COMPASSION

Wisdom and compassion need to be offered together. If we have one without the other, our caring will not be very helpful. Although not quite the same in meaning, the balancing of wisdom and compassion seems to echo the theme of structure and space. Without structure, space becomes too diffuse to be useful; without wisdom, compassion becomes unrealistic and unfocused.

If we are compassionate but not wise, we may do things out of kindness which actually make matters worse. An extreme example might be giving drugs to an addict who asks for them.

If we are wise but not compassionate we may give good advice but do so in a cold uncaring way that just hurts the person who is distressed.

The teaching on wisdom and compassion is illustrated by an old Buddhist story about an awakened being, called Quan Shi Yin. Quan Shi Yin represents compassion. According to the story, she spent many aeons (a very long time) caring for the world and trying to cure everyone's sorrows. After these many, many years she looked at the results of her work and saw that there was just as much misery in the world as there had been when she had started. When she saw this, she was so devastated that she broke into a thousand pieces.

At this point another awakened being, Amida (who here represents wisdom), put her back together. He put an eye in each of her hands so that she could see wisely when she helped people.

STRUCTURE AND SPACE IN LEARNING

The idea of structure and space is one that is not only relevant to listening and helping situations. It is also important in learning situations. If an exercise is over structured you will probably not learn much, but will just follow instructions mechanically. If an exercise has space in it, you will have to think and apply the ideas to your own experience or come up with new concepts, and so will integrate the learning.

In the last exercise, for example, you were asked to think of a situation in which you talked about personal issues. This question was very broad, and you might have come up with all sorts of scenarios. You were then given some questions as a framework for thinking more deeply about the process, but these did not have a prescribed outcome in mind. They were simply an invitation to explore. In framing this exercise, the questions needed to give space in which you could look at your particular experience. At the same time, they needed to be specific enough to stimulate your thinking. If they had been too vague, or the invitation too general, they would probably not have been much use. It the exercise had simply said 'think about this in relation to an experience you had' you might not have learned much. By giving a structure, the exercise stimulated you to come up with your own story, but gave you space to do it in your own way. Good structure provides a jumping off point from which something spontaneous can emerge.

In the same way, you will have needed to create a structure for yourself in order to do the activity. The amount that you gained from the exercise will probably have depended upon the sort of framework that you created within which to do it, and how much space you gave yourself. If you sat down with the exercise on a quiet afternoon, when you were alone in the house, you would have got more from it than if you tried to do it in between appointments on a busy day.

STRUCTURE AND SPACE IN LISTENING

The quality of attention which we bring to the task is often linked to our ability to make time and physical space for it. The same applies when we wish to create mental space to listen to another person. Creating a listening space is partly about avoiding actual interruptions, but it is also about creating mental space. Our minds are just as capable of interrupting us as our neighbours are (probably more so), so creating quiet space in the mind is a vital part of learning to listen.

Knowing that we have set aside time and feeling safe from the possibility of intrusion provides a structure in which we can relax and listen. Our mental space provides a container within which we are able to receive whatever the other person wishes to share.

In this way, creating a listening space for others is partly about offering the right physical environment, but it is also about being in the right mental state.

Our mental states, as we have seen, are conditioned by all sorts of factors. An open calm mental space is something we can start to develop through working with the conditions in our lives. We can create calm spaces in our physical environment and quiet times during our day in which to reflect and recuperate. If we can do this, we will gradually increase our capacity to offer a steady presence to others.

SACRED SPACE

The space in which we listen to another person is special. The quality of listening which we offer depends upon our ability to create an intensity of focus and appreciation, and this, in turn, is closely linked with the sort of psychological and physical space which we operate in. The qualities which are needed are like the qualities that we might associate with a sacred space.

The image of a sacred space conveys something of the special quality of the listening relationship. In offering a listening space, we engage in a process which can be awe inspiring when at its most profound. It is a process which carries a sacred mystery at its heart. Although we struggle to understand the other, and to engage wholeheartedly in listening to what they are saying, and although we may feel deeply touched and connected to their experiences, ultimately, we will always remain mysterious to one another.

The image of sacred space is something which we can reflect upon when we want to remind ourselves of the value of the work in which we are engaged. If we make this concept meaningful for ourselves, it will help us to create the calm space within us so that we can be receptive to the other.

CREATING A QUIET SPACE

You may like to bring the idea of sacred space into your home, and create a quiet haven in which to do the reflective exercises in this book. Having such a space will provide you with a refuge in which to be contemplative and relax deeply. It will be a resource in your future work, but it will also help you to develop your concentration when you do the exercises in this book.

This space will help you to build associations of calm and peace, which you can carry into your work. Making associations of this kind is called creating an *anchor*. We make a strong connection between a place (or indeed a thought or an object) and a desirable mental state, so that, by going there, or by bringing the place to mind, we create the conditions for the state of mind to return. The following exercise will help you to build this sort of association.

EXERCISE FIVE: MEDITATION ON CREATIVE SPACE
(fifteen minutes)

Find a quiet place where you will not be disturbed for fifteen minutes. Sit in a relaxed position and close your eyes.

As you sit, allow your breathing to be calm and slow and feel the chair or floor on which you are sitting supporting you. Imagine your breath flowing slowly down and around you in a curling soft cloud, holding you comfortably.

Now think of the words 'sacred space'. You can allow the words to float out of you with each breath and wrap themselves round the space in which you are sitting. As you breathe the words, allow images to come into your mind. The images that arise might be colours, shapes, places, people, or objects. Allow whatever arrives to float across your mind's eye. Do not discriminate or reject things. Just greet each one with the thought 'welcome to my sacred space'.

> When you have sat for long enough, slowly open your eyes.
> You may like to write or create art work connected with the
> image of sacred space.

Settings in which listening happens differ, and you may have
little control over the physical space you use. If you develop your
capacity to create calm mind states through this kind of exercise,
you will be able to bring a calm mind to your work, even if the
setting you are in feels less supportive.

Notice, though, how the environment in which you are
working can play a role in creating a peaceful mind state. Even in
settings where there is a lot of bustle and noise, you may be able
to make small changes which will make the environment more
welcoming and calm, inspiring and comfortable for others. Such
changes, of course, need to be suitable to the client group. What
is welcoming to a young person may be very different to the ideal
environment for an older group.

As in all things, sensitivity is all important.

Session Three

Beginnings

This session will include:

- Making initial contact
- Sitting position and body language
- Learning basic reflective listening techniques
- Learning to use open-ended questions
- Grounding exercises and meditation
- Faith and trust as a means of holding the other person

How do you start? Offering someone the space to talk may seem easy, but in practice it can sometimes be hard to get started. Even to the most confident among us, it can feel daunting to face the prospect of approaching a stranger or of offering oneself as a listening ear to people who may bring any sort of difficulty.

Depending on the circumstances in which you are working, you may have to take the initiative, or you may wait for the other person to come to speak to you. Either situation can be unnerving, especially when you are starting out.

It is, therefore, worth giving some thought to how you will begin a conversation before it happens. You may also want to get into the habit of reflecting back after the session, and thinking about what you said and what effect it had for the person you were talking with. In that way, you can learn by experience and develop your skill.

The things which you say the first time you meet with someone, or at the start of a session, are important because they set the tone for what follows. You need to let the person know that you are willing to listen and to give them the space to start to say whatever they want to say.

EXERCISE ONE: REFLECTIONS ON APPROACHING LISTENING

(five minutes)

Reflect on the way you start a conversation with someone. Think about how you might offer a listening space to someone in the setting where you are working, or where you intend to work. Run through the scenario in your mind.

- Do you approach the person?
- Do they approach you?
- How do you start the interaction?
- What do you say to introduce yourself?
- What do you say to invite them to speak?
- How direct are you in offering space to talk about personal matters?

Write down your responses.

If you are able to discuss your answers with others who are involved in this kind of work do so, but not until you have each written down your answers separately. Find out how much similarity or difference there is in your approaches.

- What effect do you think different approaches have?
- What does your approach offer?
- Does your approach put the person at ease?
- Does it open the possibility for serious discussion?
- Does it give confidence or evoke anxiety?
- Does it create an agenda, and, if so, is this helpful or limiting?

Creating the Initial Conditions

What helps someone to feel welcome to talk? If someone visits a counselling service, they are probably ready to sit down with a counsellor and begin their story immediately. Other situations are less formal and the listener may have a role to play in easing the transition from ordinary conversation to more serious interaction.

Of course, the person who comes to your agency will have their own expectations and these will colour your first contact. Their expectations may be realistic. They may understand what is on offer. But often people are not realistic or do not know what they want. They may need to be educated about what is possible and how to best use the service.

Listening situations are diverse, and whatever is included here will be limited, but let us look at some general points about the initial encounter between listener and service user. A number of factors are involved in the process. In particular you might reflect on the following things:

FIRST IMPRESSIONS

First impressions are important. The tone which is set in the first meeting is likely to colour the helping relationship for quite a while. A good first impression can make it easy to establish rapport and a bad one can take some getting over.

The impression you make is not just 'good' or 'bad'. It might communicate all sorts of things about you. Things like your dress, manner, voice tone, the context in which you meet, what you actually say and so on, all contribute to an impression which will affect not just how easy it is to establish a useful relationship, but also what sort of things the person may feel comfortable talking about.

Of course, some things, like your age, ethnicity and gender, contribute to first impressions and cannot be altered, but other things, like how you dress or your style of approach, can be changed. There are few 'right answers' in this respect, but what you do will have an effect. For example, if you are an older person working with young people you may be more able to build rapport if you dress in a low key, casual way, so long as you don't try to be too trendy. On the other hand, some older workers are very good at relating to young people because they wear 'grand-motherly' clothes and have rather old-fashioned manners. In each case, it is a mix of personality and some choices of style which creates the basis from which the relationship emerges.

The relationship which you have with the people whom you help will be different from that which they might have with someone else. Usually the relationship has the potential to be helpful in some way, whatever the chemistry. The topics you discuss or the type of interaction that follows may, however, vary. It may be easier or trickier for some people to establish a rapport in the first instance.

For these reasons, it is useful to give some thought to the impression which you are making and what possibilities it opens up, or closes. You may also need to think about whether you are the right person for this particular helping relationship. Occasionally, you may think that a particular person needs to talk to someone younger or someone of their own ethnicity or gender. If this is the case, do not be afraid to refer them to somebody else.

On the other hand, do not be too quick to make the assumption that you are the wrong person. Discuss what is best with the person you are listening to, and if they say that they want to continue to talk to you, respect their view.

THE INITIAL INVITATION

The first thing any listener or counsellor does is to offer a space in which the person can talk. As we saw in the last session, offering some kind of structure or invitation creates the space for talking. Sometimes the structure may be as simple as you sitting down and saying, "Do you want to talk?"

Other times you may need to do more; for example, suggesting that you go into another room or meet at a particular time and place. In this, there will be decisions to make about privacy and containment, as well as safety for yourself and the person you are helping.

There may also be considerations about whether, by offering the space, you are implying some sort of ongoing commitment to the person or raising their expectations of a particular outcome. There is no point, for example, in a health worker spending a long time encouraging someone to explore a number of treatment options, when most of them are not available. It is generally helpful to the person who wants to talk if you are clear in telling them what is on offer.

FEELING AWKWARD

The first encounter may go very smoothly. Often when someone is distressed they just want to pour out their troubles and if you are willing to listen, they will be very happy to talk to you. You may, in fact, be quite surprised by how easily people share personal things when you make the space for them and listen appreciatively. Sometimes you may feel after your first meeting that you have established a particularly close relationship and feel a great sense of privilege at having been trusted.

Other times, though, the initial encounter can feel difficult. You may feel awkward or lost for words, clumsy or even irritated. This sort of situation can lower your confidence when you are starting out as a listener, but it is worth remembering that everyone in a caring role has such encounters from time to time.

Often the feeling of awkwardness is not just something which you are feeling. It may also be something which the other person is feeling. Shyness and nervousness are infectious. You may simply be feeling a reflection of what the other person is experiencing. It may be an indication of your capacity to empathise with them that you are feeling it.

If you bear this in mind it will help. You might even choose to say something about the feeling. This could help you to build rapport with the other person. If you do voice the feeling, though, be careful not to inadvertently blame the other person, or to make yourself sound incompetent. When someone is already feeling anxious it is easy for them to misinterpret what is said. It may be best to say something ambiguous, which could refer to either of you, such as "It feels as if it's quite awkward talking about this."

EXERCISE TWO: NEGOTIATING A START
(ten minutes)

Think of times when you have confided in people or when you have sought out support. These might include times when you have talked with friends, or were seeing a professional counsellor or befriender.

Visualise the beginning of the conversation. What did you do or say to indicate that you wanted to share something serious? If the relationship was with a friend or in a social setting, how was the transition made from conversation to a more intense interaction?

What did the other person do and say to indicate that they were willing to listen?

Write down your memories and reflect on what you can learn from them. Do they illustrate the points made in this section?

Basic Listening Skills

The most important thing about listening to others is that you are interested in them and in their lives. If you are curious about them in a sympathetic way and want to know more, you will listen better. If you learn nothing else, this basic human concern will make you a good listener.

Other skills build upon this base, and perhaps help you to find responses and voice things that you might otherwise find hard to put into words, they help you to see beyond your assumptions and those of the people with whom you are working, and feel the unspoken elements of conversation more acutely. If, however, you lose your humanity in the process, no matter how clever you become, you will not be a good listener.

Good listening is about getting more depth of understanding in your interactions rather than just asking for more and more information. This may mean checking your perceptions and sharing your felt sense of what has been said. It may mean inviting the other person to tell you more about the situation which they are talking about. It may just mean waiting silently and patiently until they are ready to say more. Generally it does not mean telling them what you think.

In developing listening skills we learn to find out more about how it is to be the other person, experiencing the situation that they are describing, rather than simply looking for more facts about it. We imaginatively stand in their shoes and look through their eyes at the world. We feel how it is to be in their body, relating to their friends and family, living in their home, with their history. Only when we have felt this will we be ready to move on with them.

Listening to the other person is a matter of deep respect.
- We respect the person who is talking
- We respect the story they are telling
- We respect their life history, values and communities

- We respect the other people who are important to that person
- We respect the people with whom they have grievances
- We respect the healing power of listening

EXERCISE THREE: CULTIVATING RESPECT
(fifteen minutes)

Sit in the quiet space in your home. Relax and be aware of your breathing. Allow your mind and body to settle.

Bring to mind a person for whom you have concern. It might be someone who you work with, but it might equally be a friend or relative.

Imagine the person standing close to you. If you can visualise them, imagine them, perhaps in front of you. If you sense their presence, imagine them wherever you feel them to be, perhaps out of sight to the side of you. Focus your attention on the person, trying to make the sense of them stronger.

Imagine sending waves of respect and caring to embrace the person. You might like to see this as coloured light surrounding them.

Breathe deeply and allow any tension to leave your body.

Notice if you have a resistance to respecting the person. See if you can let it go.

Bring the reflection to a close and when you are ready, make notes of any observations that you made.

The most important aspect of listening is to have a basic attitude of care, interest and concern for those with whom you work. This can be developed through taking time to reflect on others' situations. On this foundation, there are various specific ways in which you can develop your skills. These methods are commonly taught on listening and counselling courses. They form a good basis for the listening process, giving you a skill-base to fall back upon. It is worth, therefore, mastering them as skills, though we are wise always to be wary of becoming mechanistic in our approach to others.

As with any skill, acquiring listening techniques takes practise. You may well find that whilst you are actually learning the skill you have to let go of the ideal of maintaining concern and respect for a while, and focus on method. For this reason, it is good to find opportunities to practise and develop your style of listening with other students who can give you feedback. In this way, you can focus on experimenting with different styles of response without worrying too much about the impact they are having. If you do not have a forum in which to practice, the listening exercises suggested here will help you to hone your skills. So, let us look at some specific methods of responding.

CHOOSING A SITTING OR STANDING POSITION

Before we look at techniques, let us first discuss the setting in which you will be working in a little more detail. In particular, if you are using some sort of consulting room or private space, or even if you are working in a more social setting, it is worth thinking about how you position furniture and how you sit relative to the person you are listening to.

I say 'sit' here, but of course there are no rules that say you have to be sitting down. In some circumstances, you may do effective listening work whilst walking together, driving in a car, or undertaking some practical task. There are no absolute rights or wrongs, but different positions can invite different sorts of relationship. This is true whether you are sitting, standing or walking.

- Placing chairs face to face gives focus to the session, but can also feel a bit too intense for some people.
- Sitting side by side in separate chairs can work well if the person is shy or inhibited, but may feel too distant in many cases. In some circumstances, being side by side may be the natural position, as when you are talking to someone whilst taking them somewhere by car or going for a walk together.
- A half-way position is probably most comfortable for most circumstances.

Most counsellors prefer a fairly upright armchair that is comfortable but not too relaxing. They will also usually choose two chairs which are identical so that they meet their client on an equal level. You may well want to do likewise if you have control over your listening environment.

Whatever your context, be aware of the effect that your relative positions have on each of you. Do they allow you to observe the person who is talking, and can the other person observe you? How easy is eye contact? Are you on a level or is one of you looking down on the other? Could you take the person's hand if appropriate? All of these factors will affect the feeling tone of our interaction. For example, if you are talking to someone who is sick in a hospital bed, you may want to pull up a chair so that you can sit at the same level as the person, rather than towering over them. You may then choose whether to place your chair so that you face them with your back to the ward, or sit beside them, sharing a view of the other beds. Each position will have a different feeling.

Where you place yourself may even affect things like how long the person expects you to be available. For example, another consideration, if you are in the hospital visiting, is that, if you sit by the bed, the person will probably expect a longer conversation than if you remain standing. None of these factors involve absolute rights and wrongs, but having an appreciation of the sort of impact which your choice of seating might have will help you to observe people's reactions and make sensible choices.

EXERCISE FOUR: REFLECTING ON SITTING POSITIONS

(ten minutes)

Think about one particular situation in which you have been involved in listening to someone.

How did you sit or stand? How did the person who was talking to you sit or stand?

Think about the impact which the position had on
• Intensity
• Eye contact
• Ease of looking at one another
• Comfort

What might the choice of position have said about levels of intimacy, expectations or style of dialogue?

Think about other ways you might choose to sit or stand and what impact a change might have on your relationship with the person. Think about other listening scenarios and compare the effects of different positions.

If you have opportunity to work with other students, experiment with using different positions in listening exercises to find out what differences it makes.

BODY LANGUAGE

Many introductory courses on listening and counselling skills pay attention to the listener's body language. Does the student sit with open posture? Do they nod in the right places? The problem with this sort of approach is that, whilst a good listener probably does indeed do these things, the body language is a manifestation of something which is going on inside the person's head, rather than something desirable in its own right. If you are being attentive, you will probably look attentive. For this reason, it is probably more important to work on developing the quality of your attention than to mimic particular postures.

This said, we all have habits of posture and sometimes a habit may be off-putting to others. Also, if you are tense or defensive in your body, this may be an indicator that there is something to be looked at either in your own attitude to the work, or in the listening relationship. Becoming more aware of your body responses is very useful. We will look more at this later in the session, in the section on grounding.

The ability to ground ourselves is valuable in giving us a 'clean slate' at the start of a session. It helps us to drop previous concerns and make space for the person we are listening to. So, at the beginning of a session it is useful to take a moment to be aware of your body feeling. If you are tense, notice it, then try to deliberately relax. It can be good to consciously breathe out slowly before you start to speak, so that you create a calm mental space, ready to receive whatever the other person wants to say.

As you go through the session, notice if tension creeps into your posture. Folded arms or crossed legs can be an indication of defensiveness. If you find yourself sitting in this way, ask yourself why you are doing so. It may be habit or nervousness, but it may also be something you are picking up from the person you are listening to. Try deliberately to relax so that you can help them to relax too.

When you are really in tune with what a person is saying,

sometimes your body language may naturally mirror that of the other person. This is a spontaneous occurrence and you may find that, if this is happening naturally, you can learn something about their experience by reflecting on your own. On the other hand, it is usually better just to try to understand how the other person is experiencing what they are saying by listening more carefully, rather than deliberately trying to mimic their movements.

REFLECTION

Perhaps the most basic and common style of intentional listening is called *reflective listening*. Reflective listening is what we often naturally do when we are interested in what someone is saying. Sometimes, with this kind of listening, the listener is simply listening attentively and giving small indications that they have heard what is being said, often in the form of non-verbal responses such as "uhuh" or "mmm", but ideally reflective listening is a more active process. The important thing with reflective listening is to listen.

More deliberate reflective responses might involve periodically checking out with the person whether you have understood what they have said. This might simply mean repeating an occasional significant word, or it might mean paraphrasing or summarising things which have been said. Doing this is a useful discipline, as it forces you to ask yourself "what have I really heard?" If you never summarise or check out your understanding, it is easy to sit looking sympathetic with a benign smile and nodding head, but to never really understand what the other person is saying, let alone the levels of meaning which lie beneath it.

Reflective listening, therefore, involves putting what you have heard, or think you have heard, into your own words. This is partly about making sure that you are in tune with the other person, but it is also about giving them the opportunity to look at what they are saying as if in a mirror. This is why it is called *reflective*. Hearing ourselves as others hear us can be a source of insight. It can be revealing, shocking or confirming.

As you become more skilled and your understanding becomes more accurate, your reflective responses may reflect not just the words actually used by the other person, but also some of the hidden layers of what they were trying to say. The language you use may be more evocative or direct than that of the person who is sharing their story.

This style of response invites the person to say more. Initially, though, as you learn to listen more attentively, focus on accurate understanding and reflection of what is actually said, rather than trying to go beyond this into layers of unspoken meaning.

REFLECTIVE LISTENING OFTEN INVOLVES SAYING THINGS LIKE:

- It sounds as if you are saying…
- Can I check if I've understood? Did you say…?
- So that's like you…
- So she went and…

When you are practising a reflective style, do not use direct questions. It is a good discipline for any student of listening or counselling skills to try practice sessions in which they never ask a direct question. Practise simply telling the person what you have heard and checking if you have understood its meaning. As you will see from the examples, many reflections are implicitly questioning, but the question is more in the area of "have I understood". They ask the person to clarify what they have already said rather than asking them to tell you more facts. Of course, the person will give you more information, but they will do this in their own time.

It is always possible to find a way of inviting the person to explore a topic further without asking a question. Questions, in this context, tend to direct the person into particular ways of thinking, which often have more to do with the listener's agenda. They also have the effect of distancing a person from the thing that they are talking about. Questions can feel like an interrogation. They make the person more likely to intellectualise or justify themselves rather than getting a feeling sense of their situation.

EXERCISE FIVE: REFLECTIVE METHODS
(forty-five minutes)

Record a short piece of speech from the radio. Ideally, choose a person who is talking about their own experience, maybe in an interview. This piece should be about five or ten minutes long.

Play back your recording, pausing the tape each time the person hesitates. At each stopping point, write down a summary of what you have just heard. Write quickly and spontaneously, as you need to practise responses which could be made in an actual interaction. When you have done this, re-start the tape.

When you have worked through the interview, replay the whole piece, listening carefully. Notice how accurate your summaries were.

Now write a short summary of the whole piece from memory.

Replay the piece a third time, again listening for meaning. Reflect on your summary and its accuracy.

OPEN-ENDED QUESTIONS

In the previous section, we saw that many questions are not really necessary for effective listening. Sometimes, however, it is useful to invite a person to share more about the topic which they are describing by using questions.

EXERCISE SIX: USE OF QUESTIONS
(thirty minutes)

Repeat the first part of the previous exercise (exercise five), using a different recording. This time with each pause write down a question you might ask to facilitate the person's exploration. When you re-start the tape, notice whether your question would have changed the person's direction of speech or whether it would have encouraged them to continue on the same track. (Do not assume that one outcome is better than the other, just notice what happened.)

EXERCISE SEVEN: OBSERVING QUESTIONS
(thirty minutes)

Listen to a professional interviewer on the radio. Notice what sort of questions they use and what effect they have. The interviewer does not necessarily have the same purpose as the listener, but you can learn quite a bit about the effects of different styles of questions on different people by listening to their styles. Again, working with a recording which you can pause and replay may be more revealing than simply listening to a piece straight through. Make notes on your observations.

In general, a basic listening approach uses what are called open-ended questions. Open-ended questions invite the person to say more, but do not impose a particular theme or direction. They tend to ask 'how' rather than 'why', and tend to invite the speaker to expand on what they are already saying, rather than moving onto new territory. Thus, an open-ended question might be:

- Can you tell me more about...?
- I wonder if you could tell me how...?
- Were there other times when that happened?
- How did that feel for her?
- If you had the choice, what options might there be?
- When they come to discuss your treatment, what will you say?

All these questions prompt the person to talk more about the topic they were discussing but leave a lot of space for their response to be in their own style.

EXERCISE EIGHT: OPEN ENDED QUESTIONS
(twenty minutes)

Maureen says: "I have to go in for an operation next week, and I'm really anxious."

Look at the following responses. Which are reflections? Which are open-ended questions and which are closed questions?
- Which day do you go in?
- You feel really anxious...
- I'm wondering what your anxiety is about.
- So it's next week...
- An operation...

- Do you often feel anxious?
- What is the operation for?
- Is there any way that we can help?

Any of these responses might be made by a listener. They are all likely to take the conversation in different directions.

Imagine that you are Maureen. Take each response in turn and write down what you would say next and how enabling or otherwise the listener's words would be.

GROUP PRACTICE OF LISTENING SKILLS

At this point, if you are working in a group, you will probably want to start practising listening skills. Skills practice can either be done in pairs, with one person talking about a concern which they have and the other person practising reflective listening or open ended questions. Alternatively, it can be done in groups of three, with a third person acting as the observer and giving feedback afterwards.

The person who is talking can talk about something from their own life. For these exercises, the subject does not need to be painful or problematic. It could be something pleasant. As a general rule it works best if it has some emotional energy. Using personal material is mostly better than acting out role plays, as it gives the listener a real experience and allows for layers of meaning to be heard (which, unless the person playing 'client' has Shakespearean talent, won't be there in a role play).

In giving feedback, it is best if the speaker and listener share their experiences first, then the observer adds their observations. Keep the focus on what the listener did and said, on how accurate that was, and on what effect the intervention had on the speaker. Do not allow feedback to become an analysis of the speaker's story. It can be useful sometimes to make an audio recording of the session so that you can review content, though this gets cumbersome if you do it too often.

If you are working through this book on your own, you may still be able to persuade someone to give you some practise of listening skills occasionally. This sort of exercise is invaluable.

Presence and Grounding

When we are with another person who is talking about something meaningful in their life, we try to give them good attention. When we achieve this, we call this quality of attention presence. Being able to offer good presence means bringing intensity and focus to our work. Presence and concentration arise naturally when we are interested. They are not techniques that can be learned in a mechanical way.

On the other hand, spending time developing our capacity to experience things more intensely, and particularly developing our body sense through meditation or grounding exercises, can be very helpful. If we have learned these skills, we will be able to intentionally bring our attention back to a calm space and, from that, to offer a peaceful presence, even when the person we are talking to is very agitated.

GROUNDING EXERCISES

One way to improve your presence is to learn grounding exercises. These exercises help you to relax and to be more in touch with your body sensation and the physical world around you. Developing awareness of our body responses is one way in which our sensitivity to others and our capacity to understand their stories increases. There is research which suggests that people who are in touch with their body sense do better in counselling.

GROUNDING EXERCISE
(twenty minutes)

You may wish to make a recording of this script so that you can play it to yourself as you practise the exercise. If you do so, speak slowly and allow spaces between the sentences and paragraphs so that you will be able to take plenty of time in following the instructions.

Start by standing with your feet shoulder width apart and your body still and well balanced. Make sure your weight is evenly distributed between your feet.

Check that your head is straight and balanced on your neck. Experiment with moving it slightly backwards and forwards to find the right point at which to settle, where it feels comfortable and your neck feel free from strain. Imagine a string tied from the crown of your head, going up to the ceiling, pulling you up straight, a bit like a puppet on a string. Relax and let the imaginary string hold you upright. Close your eyes or allow them to sink into soft focus, looking at the ground in front of you.

Now check that your shoulders are relaxed. You can hunch them up and then let them drop to release tension. Imagine your shoulders acting a bit like a coat hanger from which your arms are hung. Let your arms hang comfortably by your side. Find a place you can be still.

Allow your breath to flow evenly. Give attention particularly to the out-breath, lingering over it slightly.

Now bring your attention to your feet, as they are in contact with the ground. Feel the outline which each foot makes on the floor. You can imagine that someone has drawn a line around each of them. Keeping your upright position, allow the lower part of your body to sink a little so that the outlines increase in size. Imagine your feet filling the outlines and flowing over them. Feel the texture of the carpet or flooring as your feet make contact with them. Notice which parts of your foot are able to feel the texture of the flooring most accurately. Feel the solidity of the floor. Notice the way your body is supported by the physicality of the floor beneath it, and try to let yourself be supported further.

Now imagine your breath flowing down into that point of contact with the floor, and through it, into the ground beneath, going down into the earth, connecting you to the core of the planet. Imagine a tree with deep roots stretching down into the soil. Feel your contact with the soil through the soles of your feet, and going down into those imagined roots, and imagine your body, tall and straight, as the branches stretching up and outward, high into the blue sky under a nourishing sun.

Breathe quietly and deeply and enjoy the sense of being held.

When you are ready, you can stretch and start to move your body slowly, open your eyes and bring your attention back to the room around you. As you move, walk tall, continuing to plant your feet firmly.

Note: If you prefer, you can do grounding exercises sitting in a chair or lying on the ground. You may need to adapt the imagery which you use, but in all cases, the important principles are to intensify awareness of your contact with the ground beneath your feet or body (and of your contact with the chair, if you are sitting) and to allow yourself to be supported by it, whilst also holding an alert, but relaxed, posture. It can be useful to practice in a chair sometimes, since we often do listening work sitting down.

SIMPLE MEDITATION

The skills that you need to be a good listener are similar to those which people develop in meditation. It therefore follows that you can improve your concentration and focus as a listener by learning a meditation technique. If you do not already have a meditation practice, you might like to try sitting for ten minutes a day, doing a simple meditation exercise. In this book you will find a number of such exercises which you can use.

Use the space which you have set aside as your quiet space. Building associations of calm and concentration with that space will help you to use it as a refuge when you are working with others.

When you learn to meditate, the first thing you need to do is to sit still. Stillness in the body transfers to the mind, so that your mind becomes calmer as you sit. You do not need to sit in a standard posture, but it is good to find a position that is alert but relaxed. You might use a similar position to that which you use for grounding exercises if you practised these sitting down. Avoid hunching your chest. Let it be open so that you can breathe deeply. A very common form of meditation is to keep the attention on the breath. This is a good place to start.

To begin your meditation, focus your attention on the movement of your body. Notice the rising and falling of your ribs and belly with each breath. With each out-breath, notice the release of tension from your body. Follow each breath. Notice its first rising and its steady inflow, till your lungs are fully inflated. When your lungs have filled, the impulse to breathe out will take over. Notice how your lungs slowly release the flow of air. When the last thread of breath has left the body, you will find a natural pause occurs before the next in-breath begins. Enjoy that moment of stillness. Take several slow breaths in this way.

Now move your attention to your nostrils. Feel the breath going in and out of your nose. Try to notice the small details. What temperature is it? Which nostril takes most breath? Where do you feel the air moving? Can you feel it on your upper lip, inside your nose, or around the rim of each nostril? Holding this focus, sit and concentrate on your breathing for about ten minutes.

When you have finished, stretch gently and take your time to settle again into the space of the room before you start to move.

If you wish to vary your meditation, there are many other possible focuses for your attention. One possibility is to focus on sound. Concentrate on the sounds which you hear around you as you sit. Start by being aware of your breathing for a few minutes in order to settle your mind. Now move your focus onto the sounds which occur naturally as you sit. When you hear any sound, either in the room or outside it, imagine your breath flowing out towards the direction of the noise. Resist being distracted into thought, but simply connect each sound to a breath.

This can be a good meditation to do in places where there are noises which might distract you. You can add a thought or word to each out-breath in order to send good wishes into the world. For example when you hear each sound you might think 'love' or visualise light flowing towards the noise.

Through these exercises, you will build up your capacity to be still and to concentrate. When you listen to someone, you can bring the same focus and concentration to the interaction as you do to your meditation.

When you sit down with somebody who you are supporting, you can treat the start of the conversation a bit like the start of a meditation session. Be aware of your body as you sit down. Settle into a calm, solid sitting position. Let your body be held by the chair, but do not slouch or you will lose concentration. Take a moment to breathe out consciously before you begin. This shouldn't be obvious to the other person if you breathe smoothly and evenly. Then look at the person and smile. Invite them to speak, or make your response to what they have already said. All this only takes a few moments, but you may well notice that the person you are listening to also settles and becomes calmer. People pick up and mirror each others' body states without even noticing.

Faith and Trust

Being present for another, we offer them special space in which to talk. One way in which we can think about the presence or groundedness which we offer to others in our listening work is to think of the work as being about sharing our faith. This is not about discussing spiritual or religious ideas, or telling the other person what we think. It is more practical and, in some ways, ordinary. It is about our faith in things like the life process, the possibility of healing and whatever good influences we feel are available to people. We trust the earth we stand on and symbolically we trust the universe. Our body is less defended, less tense, and in being so is more open to others. We have faith. We trust life.

If we have a religious belief or spiritual sense, this will provide a language in which we can talk of these things with others who share our framework. We should not, however, expect that the people we support will necessarily hold the same views. It is usually inappropriate to share such views unless it is specifically in our brief.

If we have faith, this communicates to the people we listen to through our way of being. It supports their faith, even if their language for describing their faith is completely different. Faith may manifest in our confidence that the other person will sort things out in the end. Faith may manifest in a belief that there are good processes unfolding in the universe. Faith may manifest in the belief that, even if things go wrong, this person will find a way to deal with it. Faith may be grounded in a confidence that listening helps.

Everyone has faith of some kind. To be a good listener you need to harness your faith in ways that give you confidence in the process of healing. This kind of faith is not about imposing particular beliefs on the other. It is about exuding a confidence and trust which is healthy and which will convey a similar confidence and trust to the other person.

Session Four

Story and Sequence

This session will include:

- Understanding the value of telling one's story
- Recall and tracking of the story
- Direct and indirect messages
- Content and process
- Facilitative listening and stories
- The concepts of association and influence
- Repeating stories and stories behind stories
- The difficulty involved in telling the same story repeatedly
- Inspirational stories

Listening to the Story

People talk in stories. When someone comes to talk to a listener or a counsellor, they usually start by sharing stories about their life. This is not surprising. Stories are a universal way in which people communicate, and it seems that humans have told stories in every culture down the years.

Any good story is complex and has levels of meaning embedded in it. We do not necessarily have to define or even consciously recognise these meanings to be affected by them. Often they simply add a feeling of resonance, of pathos, or of satisfaction. They touch us with their nuances and with the imagery which points us towards the mysterious aspects of life without ever exposing them fully.

In the same way, the stories which people tell about their lives tell us about the world which they inhabit and the way that they perceive things. They give us clues about aspects of the person which are hidden and about the deeply held convictions which drive and nourish their lives. When we listen to someone's story we are given privileged entry into their world. We are invited to see through their eyes.

Stories, then, have meaning on different levels. Here are some:

At a simple level, the story which a person tells us gives us information about particular events, and characters who are significant in their life.

The story also tells us about the way the person sees life in general. It shows us what is important to them, and how they perceive particular events. It allows us to look at the world through their eyes.

The story may well be symbolic of other stories. A story about the death of a pet may also be a way of expressing grief over the death of a loved one. A story about a success at work may say something about what the person wants to achieve on a bigger scale in life.

Stories can be ways of communicating indirectly. They can be about telling the listener things which are hard to say directly. They may test trust or communicate secrets.

EXERCISE ONE: EXPLORING STORY THROUGH DIFFERENT RECORDING METHODS
(half an hour)

If you are working with this book on your own, find a programme on the radio or television in which a person is telling a personal story. The story should be about five to ten minutes long. Record it so that you can listen to it again or use a 'listen again' feature on the internet. Listen to it carefully, giving good attention to what is being said, and to the voice tone of the speaker.

If you are in a group, work in pairs. One person, be the speaker, and the other person, the listener. The listener should use reflective listening and open-ended questions to help the speaker to tell their story. The story can be anything about yourself and your life. Preferably talk about something which you have some feelings about, but not something which is very difficult for you, as you are going to look at the listening style and discuss how the session went. (*Talk for five minutes.*)

After the session, use the following recording methods to explore how well you remembered what was said. If you are working with a partner, do not talk or look at each other's page. The person who told the story can do the recording as well as the listener:

1. Turn your page sideways. Draw a line across the page to represent the story, beginning on the left and ending on the right. Along the line, write words and phrases that give the detail of the story as it unfolded. Try to fill out as much detail as possible. (*Three minutes.*)

2. Take a new sheet of paper and write down all the characters in the story. You might include significant objects too. Spread them out over the page, putting them in relation to one another intuitively. For example, you may feel two people (A and B) know each other well and a third party (C) didn't know either of the others, so you might place A and B close together and C somewhere else on the page. Next to each character jot down what you know about them. (*Three minutes.*)

3. Using a different coloured pen, mark both diagrams with any feelings or intuitions that you had relating to the story. What did you feel might have been going through the

speaker/listener's mind? What might people or events represent for the speaker? Did you have a sense of why they were significant? (*Three minutes.*)

Listen to the story again, or compare notes with your partner to check out your memories and your hunches about what might have been going on. If you are working in pairs, you may notice that the speaker picked up things that the listener was thinking but not saying. This may have influenced the way she or he continued to tell the story.

What is Really Being Said?

Stories are not always to be taken on face value. Although they may apparently be about other people or places, often, unknown to the listener, they may also be about communicating things to the listener which are difficult to say directly. People tell stories for reasons and commonly the story has a 'message' embedded in it. For example, if someone tells you about their aunt who felt very hurt by someone she trusted, they may also be saying to the listener "please do not hurt me", or even, "what you said last week hurt me." If someone tells a story about how he achieved something, he may really be saying "I'm not as pathetic as I look at the moment, I can do well sometimes." We need to listen to what people are saying with an open view and allow their stories to speak to us of other levels of meaning.

Sometimes, when people tell us their stories, they may be doing so as a way of testing out whether they can trust us. When we tell someone something personal, we notice how that person responds and we assess whether we can trust them with more personal information. We may not be aware that we are doing this, but this is how most relationships develop. By small steps, each person gradually tests the ground and so builds more trust.

When we really listen to a person's story, it becomes apparent that there is generally more being said than first meets the eye. There may be all manner of underlying themes and agendas. When we do this, we start to understand the complexity of human communication. At this point we can get confused, but really we have all been communicating on these complex levels all of our lives.

Most of the time people are not consciously aware of the different cues that other people give in their ordinary conversations. They think of the indirect messages which they pick up as their intuition or as hunches. As we begin to listen more carefully, we can continue to trust our feelings and intuitions about what is going on, but we learn to bring more into consciousness, so that we can respond more effectively to people's half-voiced needs.

As a listener, then, the first task is to learn to follow the storyline and keep track of the main events and characters. In addition, we can also reflect on the way that the person is telling the story. These two elements, the story line and the way that the story is told, go hand in hand. They are sometimes referred to as *content* and *process*. Notice that in exercise one, the notes which you made in the first colour pen were to do with content and notes that you made in the second colour were to do with process. As your skills develop you will become increasingly aware that both these strands are going on at the same time.

CONTENT	PROCESS
The story line	How the story is told
Facts	Emotional tone
Characters	Language
Events	Use of images
Scene being described	Meaning communicated to listener

Counsellors pay a lot of attention to process, since it is through the process that we learn more about how the person construes their world and what they are really trying to say to us. As a listener, it is less important to be thinking about process, but there will be times when paying attention to how the person is talking, as well as what they are saying, will help you to avoid falling into the more obvious pitfalls. For example, as we saw above, if the story is really intended to tell you something (and the intention may not be a conscious one) it may be much more valuable for you to understand and acknowledge the hidden message than to simply go on finding out more and more detail. It may be better to realise that you hurt the person's feelings than to discover more about Auntie.

This said, much human communication is indirect, and we pick up all sorts of nuances from people, and respond to them, without ever realising it. As long as you are listening with a warm and honest intention, the indirect messages will probably look after themselves most of the time.

Helping Someone to Tell Their Story

In the last session we introduced the basic skills of reflective listening and open-ended questions. These will be helpful in facilitating someone in telling their story. The main thing which you need to do as a listener is to be interested, but having some skills will help you to express this.

People who seek support have often spent some time building up to the point when they will ask for help, and during that time they may well have run through their story time after time in their head. When at last they have the opportunity to tell it, they may simply pour out what is already there, using well rehearsed words, or they may find that, in giving voice to the story, it is somehow different and their perspective on the events changes just because the story is being heard by someone else.

WITNESSING

Having a witness to our stories can be a very important experience. People who have suffered trauma can feel desperately alone with what they have gone through. Someone who is a refugee or victim of abuse may simply need you to listen, and in doing so, to acknowledge the pain they are recounting. So, witnessing is an important function for the listener. Do not feel that you necessarily have to do anything other than sit with the person and give your full attention.

EXERCISE TWO: WITNESSING STORIES AND MEDITATION
(half an hour)

Find a radio programme or television interview in which a person is talking at some length about an experience which was traumatic for them. You are likely to find such interviews in current affairs programmes. If possible, make a recording of it.

Go into a quiet space with your recording and listen intently to what the person is saying, imagining that you are actually with them, and witnessing their experience. Try to stay present both to their account, and to the feelings which it arouses in you.

When the interview has finished, sit quietly and observe the reaction you have to what you have heard. Notice any body sensation which has stayed with you. Make notes about your experience.

ENGAGEMENT

Whilst sometimes the speaker needs you to act as an unobtrusive witness, other times the speaker welcomes a listener who is more active. In particular, if the story is one which has been told many times, the speaker may be looking for a new way of seeing the situation or a different perspective. A listener may influence the direction of the story by:

- Being interested in details about characters or events or places.
- Asking for more information about things which seem important.
- Asking for more details about things that are being omitted.
- Asking what happened before or after the main event.
- Asking about what different situations felt like for the people involved.
- Asking what people might have been thinking when they did certain things.

Recall and Tracking

One of the challenges for the listener can be to recall the elements of a long and complex story. When stories are very complicated, you may need some help in holding onto all the details. Do not be afraid to ask the person to go back over something they have already said if they have lost you. It is more important that you understand them than that you appear to have listened perfectly. Sometimes they may have skipped over something important and the invitation to go back and clarify things will help them to see a new aspect to the issue.

Another way of clarifying things can be to invite the person to use a sheet of paper and show you what they are talking about. For example, if there are a lot of family members, you might ask the person to draw a diagram or a family tree so that you can be clear who is who. If there were a long sequence of events you might invite them to draw a time-line and mark the events on it. Alternatively you might draw these diagrams yourself, asking the person to show you how to do it. We have already used drawing exercises which offer ways to represent groupings of people or histories: timelines and net diagrams. They are ways for exploring experiences which can be infinitely adapted.

Using a reflective style of listening helps you to recall. Do not be afraid to be active in checking your understanding by summarising what you have heard. This will keep you engaged with the process. You may need to *interrupt* sometimes to do this, but it is important to do so if the story is getting complicated, so that you can check you are still alongside one another. Active listening does not necessarily follow social norms. Interrupting is better than losing track of what the person who is talking to you is saying. Don't be afraid to say, "Hang on, can we go back a minute?" or "Hold on, didn't you just say…"

EXERCISE THREE: HEARING STORIES
(indeterminate)

Take opportunities to listen to people telling their stories. This might mean engaging in conversation with people you might not usually talk to, like the person at the bus stop, the shop keeper or tradesman, or people at the place where you work.

Notice how readily people will tell you stories about their lives and how you can encourage them by showing interest and being facilitative. Practise using open-ended questions and reflective responses.

One particular skill that is important when you are listening to people's stories is the ability to recall things which were mentioned and then apparently forgotten. This skill is called *tracking*. It is often the element in the story which is skipped over which turns out to be a significant factor in the account, so remembering it and asking about it later can be very helpful. People sometimes avoid looking at things which are difficult and make short cuts in their minds, missing out vital details. To help a person retrace such thoughts, you might ask "so what *did* happen to Auntie Mary?" or "so what did you do that day when you bunked off school?" Often the answer will throw new light on the issue which the person is talking about.

Myth and Common Stories

In our cultural heritage there are many common stories and myths. Some of these are traditional folk tales which we have learned since childhood. Others are more modern versions; urban myths and stories from the popular press.

Such stories have a function in society, giving us a sense of our common inheritance and passing down wisdom and ethical ideas through the generations. They convey the culture of a society and communicate its values. They are a rich resource which sadly seems to be diminishing, at least in its more traditional forms.

Groups and families also have their stories, and these serve a similar function to the myths of society at large, creating a sense of common identity and bonding and reflecting important aspects of the shared world view and history. Families talk about the disastrous Christmas when everyone got sick, or the hilarious exploits of children when they were young. They may also talk about their escape from the home country when an oppressive regime took over, or the achievements of Grandad in setting up his own business. Such stories bring family members together and remind them of the family view of what is important in life.

EXERCISE FOUR: FAMILY STORIES

(twenty minutes)

What stories were told in your family when you were growing up?

What sort of message do you think they were conveying to family members who heard and repeated them?

Write down some of the stories which you recall.

When people tell their stories, they may be offering more than just a personal sharing. They may be bringing the values and identities of the groups with which they identify into the conversation. They may be drawing on the support of their culture and welcoming you into it, or conversely, they may be excluding you by hiding the real point of the story. Groups often tease the newcomer with references to stories which are never explained.

ALLUSION TO MYTH

Other times, people draw on stories and myth that are in the common culture as ways of communicating personal material. The myth provides a metaphor for the person's situation, which is redolent with associations. Mostly this kind of use of myth and folk tale happens by allusion rather than by actually recounting the tale. We might refer to someone as 'a bit of a Cinderella' or 'a fairy godmother'. This works so long as everyone knows the original story and shares the same understanding of its meaning. Sometimes, a speaker will assume that you know a story; for example, referring to a film or celebrity whom you do not know. You may need to probe deeper to understand the meaning of the allusion.

The use of allusion, itself, may add a layer of complicity to the conversation, as it demonstrates the shared culture. How much complicity is involved may depend upon how common or obscure the allusion is. If the person speaking is talking about a musician you have never heard of, this may be an invitation to join the inner-circle by getting to know more, or it may be a sort of test to see if you are part of the same culture. It may even be a way of excluding you and demonstrating your difference.

Because myths deal with powerful issues, such as life and death, jealousy and revenge, even casual allusions can hint at darker forces which a person may be wary of voicing directly. Myth and story can provide a powerful, expressive medium and there may be times when you can draw on it as a source of inspiration for creative work or drama, which can form a basis for community groupwork and individual personal exploration.

Association

In session two, we looked at the way that many conditions contribute to any situation or event. What we say on any occasion is conditioned by a whole lot of factors. These might include things like our history, our present circumstances, the environment we are in, or the people we have been talking with recently.

One particular type of conditioned relationship, which affects the way our minds work, is called *association*. Put simply, this theory suggests that one thought follows on from the last. Each idea is conditioned by the previous one. This means that what we say is conditioned by whatever happened immediately before we said it. This might be the thing that we said previously, or something that someone else (like the listener) said, or it might be conditioned by something that happened previously or by something which caught the person's eye.

Thinking about the process of association can be useful for two reasons.

Firstly, it may help us to understand why someone is telling a particular story and what meaning it might have for them. Sometimes it can give a context to something which might otherwise seem troubling. We might realise that what is being said is less serious than it, at first, seemed. For example, if Susan starts to talk about an aunt who died recently, without knowing the context we might think she was about to express her grief, but if we realise that actually the conversation is about cooking and her aunt was a very good cook, we will be less likely to make assumptions of this kind. We may listen more carefully to hear what Susan is really feeling and saying.

Other times, we may see that the casual comment has greater significance. When Andy comments that the weather is cold, we might think nothing more of it unless we realise that earlier he was talking about his grandmother who is very frail.

Secondly, when we understand the type of process that is involved in association, we may realise that behind the story is a hidden thought or another story which has not been voiced at all. Mostly, we can only guess that the hidden element is there, but if we have a strong intuition of it, it might be useful to ask tentatively about it.

This sort of hidden process is something that can often be observed in people's body language. Most of us recognise when someone else is lost in their thoughts or distracted from a conversation. We can use a reflective style of response for such occasions too. We might say "It looks as if you are a long way away!" or "I felt you drifted off then." or "It looks as if there is more to this than you are saying." Such reflections, if gently said, can invite the person to be aware of the hidden thoughts and voice them if they wish.

The stories that people tell when they are talking to a listener, may be told because the story itself is very important to them, but they may also be conditioned by the circumstances and told because some immediate trigger has led to a thought process. As humans, we enjoy the process of talking and establishing intimacy with others, and the subject matter of conversation may sometimes be little more than 'something to talk about'. The real purpose may be simply having a conversation rather than a concern with the subject which is being discussed.

This can be true even of seemingly significant material. For example, if someone walks into a room and sees a poster on the wall about Alcoholics Anonymous, he might well talk to you about his drinking habits even if he is not particularly concerned about them. Through the process of *association*, the immediate environment, which we are conversing in, can distort what is discussed. Realising this can prevent the listener from rushing in like the cavalry to try to solve a person's 'problems' when they are really not his central concern.

EXERCISE FIVE: ASSOCIATION AND AGENDAS
(five minutes)

Think about a conversation which you had today in which you were the first to speak or introduced a new topic.

What did you say first? What led you to say that?

Might it be:
- What another person said?
- What happened before you came into the room?
- What you saw when you came into the room?
- What you always say in that sort of setting?
- What you thought the person you were speaking to might like to hear (based on your previous experience)?

Reflect over other conversations using the same prompt questions

---

ASSOCIATION IN THE LISTENING RELATIONSHIP

Another aspect of the theory of association can be observed in the listening relationship itself. When we listen to people, we ourselves are strong conditioning factors for them. The person who is talking to us usually has us in their line of sight as they start to speak, so our presence may well colour what is said.

People may talk to different listeners about different things. They may talk to an older woman about one aspect of their life and a young man about another. This is a natural part of human interaction. There is little you can do to change this, but there will be occasions when being aware of the effect that your presence is probably having may be useful.

We can have a strong impact on the content of what people talk to us about. This can particularly be the case if you are listening in a role which carries a popular stereotype and has popular associations. For example, if you are a chaplain and wear a dog collar this is bound to affect what people say to you. If you are a nurse, you are likely to find people focus on their concerns about health. If you are a social worker, people will be wary of telling you certain things. All three people may listen to the same patient in a hospital and hear completely different stories. This may seem obvious, but can be forgotten sometimes.

Also, the observation that *association* colours what people say becomes useful if we think about the second type of understanding which comes from this theory. It may be that the dog collar or the nurse's uniform conditions a hidden response which, in turn, conditions a story that is told.

The missing link in this chain is the hidden story, and this may have great significance for the person. If the patient tells the chaplain a favourite poem, it may be a simple sharing, but it might be that the person is afraid that they are dying and is thinking of what poems might be read at their funeral. They may associate 'chaplain' with 'priest', and 'priest' with 'funerals'.

You will not reach such a line of understanding just by

reasoning or even by empathic skills, but being aware that your presence might condition such thoughts may make you more sensitive to clues which the person gives in the manner of what they say. Recognising your own part in the interaction, and the chain of association, which it might evoke, may help you to better understand the subtle levels in what a person is communicating and to reach an intuition of the hidden story.

EXERCISE SIX: DIFFERENT THERAPISTS, DIFFERENT STORIES
(twenty minutes)

Take an old magazine or colour supplement. Tear out five or six pictures of people. Choose pictures where you can see the person's face and select pictures of adults of a variety of ages and backgrounds. Try to find pictures of people who you could imagine meeting on the street rather than images from fashion shots.

Take each picture in turn and put it in front of you. Sit and look at the person and imagine meeting them in a listening relationship where they were the listener.

If you were going to talk to them, what might you talk to each of them about? What story might you tell about yourself? What would you feel inhibited to mention?

Make some notes about the differences

Repeating Stories

As we go through life, we tend to think and act in habitual ways.

It is surprising how often we end up repeating the same stories over and over again, simply substituting different people and places in the key roles. Maybe we keep falling out with men who are in authority over us. Maybe we keep falling in love with people who have similar personalities. Maybe we always seem to end up living in similar types of housing situations, with all the same problems repeating over and over again. Whatever our story is, it can be uncanny how we seem to keep repeating the same life script.

EXERCISE SEVEN: REPEATING SCRIPTS
(half an hour)

Think about your own life history. You might like to do another lifeline diagram, marking on the important relationships which you have had and significant changes, such as career moves or changes of housing. Can you identify stories or scripts that you have experienced repeating in your life? Is there any connection between your relationships and the life changes, for example? Do you have similar patterns of relationship, either in the type of person you are attracted to or in how the relationship develops or ends?

Explore what sort of patterns you tend to follow and how they are similar or different each time round. Are there patterns of behaviour you used to repeat which you no longer repeat? If so, what caused you to move on from that particular 'story'?

It can be useful to recognise the repeating patterns in our personal stories, because recognising the pattern can sometimes help us to get out of the loop. On the other hand, such patterns are surprisingly persistent, and awareness on its own is rarely enough to prevent them recurring. Sometimes we might understand something which lies behind the pattern, whether this is a need or a way of seeing the world, or, more often, we simply change in such a way that the function which the pattern was fulfilling is no longer needed.

Unhelpful Stories

In general, when we listen to people, we encourage them to tell their stories and, through this, we help them to gain confidence and develop trust. Sometimes, though, a person may have a habit of 'telling stories' and this may be a way of avoiding talking about other things which are more meaningful. Perhaps there are things in their life which are frightening or threatening to voice. Or maybe they have developed a habit of telling stories because they are shy or because it has made them popular in the past. Tom repeats his tales of his days in the RAF, during the war. He is old and frail now, and few people would believe he was once a pilot. Bernadette talks about her son in Australia, who got a first class degree five years ago. She does not want to tell people that he rarely writes and that she misses him dreadfully.

If a person tells the same story repeatedly or talks in a monotonous way, so that it is hard to feel engaged with what is being said, it may be that the person is stuck in a story loop. Just listening to the story again may not help.

Often the best way out of such a loop is to listen more carefully. There is usually something in the story which is significant, but it may take careful listening to hear the point. Sometimes it is also a matter of getting to a stage where there is enough trust in the helping relationship that the person feels able to share more. When a person really feels heard, they may start to tell you new things and move on from the story loop.

Sometimes, however, you may need to gently suggest a new direction or ask a question that changes the flow a little.

EXERCISE EIGHT: BEHIND THE SCENES
(ten minutes)

Mina talks about her teenage daughter, Parvina, again. She is critical of Parvina for her tastes in Western clothes and music and because she does not help in the home the way an Asian daughter should. Mina has told you the same things on each occasion when you have seen her. Although you listened sympathetically the first time, you are feeling frustrated that nothing you say seems to help.

What sort of things might lie behind Mina's story? Why do you think she keeps moaning to you about her daughter? What might you say which might help her to talk about her concerns more directly?

Inspirational Stories

As we have already seen, the stories which people tell may be deeply significant for them in conveying their sense of community, culture, or personal meaning. We all have our stories. Some are ones which we have carried for years, reiterating to anyone who will listen. Others lie at the back of our minds, emerging in our attitudes and thought patterns.

To this stock of old stories, we are constantly adding new material. Things we are told or perceive become integrated into our fund of ideas. Stories that we are exposed to, enrich our experience. Even sad or distressing stories may touch our hearts and draw out our capacity for compassion and fellow feeling.

This being so, we do not need to be too ready to protect people from each other's stories. Sharing in groups can be very valuable for people who have experienced trauma, not just because they have opportunities to be heard, but also because they can hear the stories of others.

In such stories too, there is often much that is inspiring. The courage which people show in the face of adversity, and the spirit which uplifts people even when things seem darkest, may be a source of encouragement and positive energy.

Inspiration is an important source of mental well being, so we will return to it in future sessions, but in the context of this session, it is useful to think about ways in which people's stories reflect the sources of inspiration in their lives and, in consequence, ways in which these can be enhanced and supported.

MEDITATION EXERCISE: SENDING LIGHT
(twenty minutes)

Begin your meditation by spending five minutes repeating the grounding exercise, which you learned in the last session. You may like to stand to do this. Focus on your sense of connection to the earth and your feeling of strength.

Now sit down and feel your connection to the earth. Bring the same sense of calm into your body in the sitting position as you had when standing.

Recall the person whose story you listened to in exercise two. Think of the account and what happened to the person, particularly focusing on the parts of the story which touched you emotionally.

Imagine the person sitting close to you. Imagine sending positive wishes to them. You might like to picture these as rays of coloured light.

When you are ready, bring your meditation to a close. You may repeat this meditation on other occasions, reflecting on people whom you have met through your work as a listener.

Session Five

A World of Objects

This session will include:

- The idea that our states of mind are conditioned by objects
- The use of objects as a basis to help people talk more deeply about their lives
- Symbolic objects and objects which offer support
- Creating anchors for positive feelings by working with objects
- Identifying significant people or places in the speaker's story
- Reflecting objects not feelings
- Offering containment when emotion becomes too strong

We live in a world of *objects*. The word 'objects' is used here in a somewhat technical way. It means any people, places, possessions, and other things which are significant in our lives. The things which we see, or which we experience through other senses, affect our moods, our thoughts and our expectations. When we see a rose flowering, we probably feel happy. When we hear a baby crying, we may feel irritated or sympathetic. When we smell fresh bread, we may feel nostalgic or hungry. When we see a sunset, we may feel inspired or sleepy. When we see a good friend, we may feel love or be reminded of things we did together in the past. So our mind is constantly being caught and transformed by things.

We can say that *the mind is conditioned by the object of attention*. What we see conditions our emotional response. We react to a thing that we see with emotional energy.

At the simplest level, we react in one of three ways. We like it or don't like it or we feel neutrally towards it. Put another way, we identify with it or we reject it. We dwell on it in our thoughts or we push it away and distract ourselves from it.

At a more complex level, we have particular associations with it, so that one object can evoke whole worlds of images and ideas. We see a picture and suddenly our mind has run off into all manner of memories or thoughts. In this way, one object conjures up other objects, which, in turn, evoke responses in us.

<table>
<tr><td>OBJECTS ATTRACT
OR REPEL US</td><td>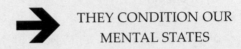</td><td>THEY CONDITION OUR
MENTAL STATES</td></tr>
</table>

The objects which appear in our minds are just as potent as those which we see in real life. Even when we are thinking, our mind is still affected by objects. The thoughts we have evoke images which evoke reactions. If I ask you to think of a person you are fond of, you will have one set of responses. If I ask you to think of someone you had an argument with, you will have a different reaction. The person whom you thought of was not actually present in either case, and yet you probably, in some sense, saw or experienced their presence.

Indeed the strength of your reaction probably related closely to the degree of 'reality' in your perception of them. If you imagined them strongly, either seeing them with your mind's eye or feeling them with you, you probably had a much more feeling response than if you thought of them in a more abstract way.

We can refer to these imagined figures as *mind-objects*. When we are listening to people who are telling their stories, they will share with us many mind-objects. Sometimes the people whom they talk about will be very present in the room as we listen. Other times they will be less so. We will sense the difference, as we notice the amount of feeling evoked.

When we listen to people, they tell us about the objects which are significant in their lives. They talk about things like:

- People who they know or have known
- Places
- Things that belong to them or to other people

They also talk about objects which are more abstract like

- My pension
- The council
- My views on the current issues of the day
- God

Recognising objects which are physical is often easier, but abstract things like ideas or concepts can be just as powerful in conditioning our mental states.

As you will have noticed, many objects have 'my' implied in their name. We identify with some objects and this makes them very important to us. Other objects may be associated with other people so may be significant for other reasons. We might have special feelings for 'Grandmother's best china' or 'Grandpa's garden shed'. In this way, everyday objects may become symbolic of the people with whom they are associated, and thus, may be invested with powerful psychological energy.

Those things which we identify with ourselves tend to be particularly powerful, because, being human; we tend to be rather self-interested!

Talking about Objects

In the last session we saw how people might tell their stories and, through those stories, might explore the meaningful aspects of their lives. Within the stories which people tell, objects often take on great significance, symbolically resonating with the heart of the drama and with the people who are most precious within it. Charles talks about his record collection and how he brought some of the disks with him when he first came to Britain in the sixties. The records remind him of his home country and those early days settling into a new life.

Such objects often reside in our everyday world so that, through the ordinary objects which we see day to day, we live out our dreams, feel our loved ones around us, and see our stories replayed. We use the tea-set, play the records, or read the books.

Working with such objects has many facets, but one important aspect is the connection it brings between the speaker and significant people in their life. The apparently mundane object links the person to other significant objects, such as the people and places which have been important to them.

One way of helping someone to talk about their life in a meaningful way, therefore, is to notice an object which is significant for them and encourage them to talk about it. This can be done as an exercise, but more often in listening relationships, it is introduced in a more natural, conversational way. This book will give you exercises which will help you to try out this way of working for yourself, but, once you have grasped the basic methods, as a listener you will probably find ways to facilitate this kind of exploration spontaneously.

Opportunities are all around us. For example, if you notice that someone is wearing a distinctive piece of jewellery, you might comment on it and ask more about it. It may have no particular significance, but on the other hand, it may take you into a meaningful conversation about the person who gave it or a family member from whom it was inherited. People often wear jewellery that has personal meaning.

You might equally comment on something else, which the

person has with them, like a book they were carrying, a card or picture on their desk or bedside table, or an unusual bag. Be interested. Obviously there is a balance to be struck between interest and intrusiveness, but with sensitivity you may provide opportunities for the person to share important memories and stories.

If you are in a role where you visit people in their own homes, there will be many opportunities for this kind of conversation. As a befriender or support worker you will probably notice all sorts of objects which turn out to have great personal importance. Asking about these may well open the door for the person to share important personal experiences and connections.

An obvious source of conversation of this kind might be photographs. Most people have some family photos in their homes, or pictures of places they have visited or of friends. You might ask the person about the pictures which they have around them. This can be done in a conversational way, as a casual enquiry allows the person to respond in a light-hearted manner, but be prepared to follow up your initial enquiry with a more serious question if the person seems ready to talk in more depth about the people depicted.

Other things which might catch your attention could include antique objects, which might have a history in the family, trinkets and mementoes, or children's art work. You might also comment on changes in the decoration of the room since your last visit. The choice of colours or furnishings may have personal meaning, and there is often a story behind the decision to redecorate.

Of course, some objects have great emotional importance. You cannot always know in advance what something means to the person, so do not be surprised if people sometimes express grief or regret in response to such an enquiry. If you make your initial approach lightly, the person is only likely to share what they feel comfortable to talk about.

EXERCISE ONE: EXPLORING A SIGNIFICANT OBJECT

(twenty minutes)

If you are working in a group:

Work with a partner. If you are the person who is going to talk first, choose an item which you have on your person today. It might be a piece of jewellery or clothing or something you have in your pocket or handbag. Choose your item intuitively. Do not deliberately choose the one with greatest significance, but do talk about something that you feel some affinity for.

The listener can facilitate, using questions and reflections, and encouraging the speaker to explore associations, images, feelings and thoughts that arise from the object. You can start by simply describing it and see where that takes you. In this instance, questions can be more specific. You are trying to discover the speaker's associations with the object, so details may be helpful. You might ask things like:

- Where did you buy it?
- What was going on at the time?
- Who gave it to you?
- What did she say?
- Why did you choose that one rather than the other one?
- What colour would you have preferred?
- Where would you like it to go when you die?

(These questions are examples of the types of things which you might ask. They are not intended as instructions about what to say! Be guided by your own curiosity and intuition.)

If you are working on your own:
Walk around your house and choose a small object which catches your attention. It could be anything, so long as it is portable.

Take your object into your quiet space and sit with it in front of you. Take a large sheet of paper and write down on it whatever comes to mind in association with the object. You can use the questions above as prompts, or just free associate.

Use alternate periods of silent contemplation, in which you allow the object and any images which come to mind associated with it to float through your thoughts, and periods of spontaneous writing.

When you have finished, reflect back over the process and what has emerged from it.

EXERCISE TWO: CONVERSATIONS ABOUT OBJECTS
(indeterminate)

Take opportunities to have conversations with people about significant objects in their worlds. Comment on things which you observe as they speak and notice how willing (or not) people are to share their personal stories about their possessions with you.

One Thing Leads to Another

As a person talks about the significant objects, as in exercise one, you may well find that the conversation reveals other significant people and moments in their life. One object hides a series of other objects and you can continue to enquire into these, bringing each, in turn, to life by asking more about it. In other words, a story unfolds.

Conversely, stories can be seen as a series of objects presented one after the other.

That ring belonged to your mother...

Tell me more about your mother...

Your mother lived in Birmingham during the war...

Tell me more about Birmingham during the war...

There were air raids...

Tell me more about being in an air raid... What did she see...? Where did she live...? What was her house like...?

As we become more skilled at listening, we learn to spot significant objects and not to hurry over them, but to ask more. There are always many possibilities, but it may well be better to spend an hour talking about an afternoon visiting mother in the nursing home than to hear the whole family history if the person's real concern lies with their mother.

On the other hand, at other times it can be very helpful to hear the whole story. In getting the overall picture of a person's situation, we can become more aware of the range of stresses and possibilities which open up to them.

EXERCISE THREE: SECONDARY OBJECTS
(fifteen minutes)

Taking a piece of paper, draw the object which you discussed in exercise one in the middle. To the left of it, draw or write all the other objects which were mentioned in your enquiry into the original object. Mark those which seemed significant, about which you might have asked more.

To the right of the object, draw or write all the feeling responses which you, or your partner if you were working in a pair, had to the object.

Reflect on the relationship between the original object and the other objects which emerged during the exploration. Reflect on the relationship between all of these and the feeling responses.

At what points were the feeling responses strongest? How did they change as different objects emerged?

Symbolism and Objects

One of the reasons why working with objects is so useful is that the objects ground the person's attention in real tangible things. Whilst one is talking about something in a more abstract way, it is possible for feelings to be more diffuse. When we hold an object in our hand or touch it on a shelf, we feel its reality. The object then becomes a bridge between the concrete world of things and the hidden world of thoughts, feelings, beliefs and intuitions.

SYMBOLIC OBJECTS

Whilst the original object which you explore may be tangible, it often emerges that this object is significant because it is symbolic of another object. The ring is not significant in itself. It is important because it was given by a lover. The photograph is just a piece of glossy paper, but it depicts the family on a happy occasion. Each object is a tangible token of something which is very precious to the person. Its power is in its ability to hold the memory of a time, a place, a presence.

When an object is symbolic, it becomes a sort of shorthand for the really significant aspect of what it represents. It can be carried around, placed where it can be viewed regularly, or taken into difficult situations. In this, it becomes a distillation of the presence of the person or phenomenon which it stands in for. We can take our partner with us when we travel by wearing their ring. We can hold our children close to us, even after they have grown up, by having their photograph in our purse.

Sometimes, however, this miniaturization also holds pain at a bearable distance. The small memento creates a link to the dead person, but somehow assuages the grief, at least in part, by placing it in a physical space. Just as people will weep when they visit the grave of a loved one and then return to ordinary life, leaving the emotion behind, so too the object becomes a kind of repository of grief which can be taken out and put away, and its small size allows for small expressions of the misery; measured doses of what might otherwise be overwhelming.

RELIGIOUS ITEMS

A particular example of the symbolic object is the religious item which is cherished by the practitioner of a particular faith. Whether it is a cross or a holy picture, a book or a strand of cotton, prayer beads or a religious figurine, the religious artefact is an example of an object which has become the container of a particular set of responses, associations and feelings.

Such items are very significant for people and it is easy to underestimate their role, particularly at times of crisis. When the person is beyond words, perhaps in sickness or nearing death, such objects give great comfort and inspiration.

Here again, it is not the object itself which is significant, but the meaning which is placed in it. There are exceptions as some objects are seen as carrying power in themselves. Mostly, though, it is the spiritual value which the object represents which is really the source of comfort.

Some things carry religious or spiritual symbolism which may seem unorthodox or trivial, yet are still potent for the person concerned. It may be easy to be dismissive of the St Christopher pendant, the lucky stone, or wishing upon the first star, but for some people such symbolic objects may be just as potent as a cross or a sacred picture. Listening to the personal importance and symbolism, and respecting it, is more important than adhering to traditional ideas and doctrines. The object may reflect a faith which is just as sincere as that of the more sophisticated practitioner.

CREATING SYMBOLIC OBJECTS

Whilst many objects naturally acquire significance because of their connection with people, places or events, it is sometimes helpful to deliberately create an object which can be a source of support. People create symbolic objects all the time by building associations. We can harness this process.

If you have been working in a group, and using the stone passing method which was suggested in session one as a way of sharing, the stone which has been passed around the group may well have taken on special significance for you as a group member. It may have come to represent the group spirit in some way.

Similarly, if you have created a quiet space in your home in which to work, this too has probably taken on a special significance and associations for you and objects in it may likewise have become special. We can deliberately cultivate certain objects as sources of support. We have already talked about the way a place can be developed as an *anchor* for feelings of calm and refuge in session one. Objects can be similarly used as anchors.

If you are working with somebody who suffers from a lot of anxiety, you might invite her to choose a pebble, to represent peacefulness. Choosing the right pebble would, in itself, be a process which might take time, and might have associations with walking in the garden or on a beach, say. You might then work with relaxation exercises or guided meditations to create an association between the stone and a peaceful state of mind. Once this has happened, the person will be able to hold the stone and in doing so draw on the association, bringing back the feelings of peace. The stone can be carried in a pocket as a concrete reminder of the peaceful state, which can help in re-accessing it.

For someone who suffers from anxiety, creating such an anchor for calm or positive feelings can be very valuable. If you do this kind of work, however, remember that in creating the object you are probably not simply creating something which represents peace. The object will probably also become a strong reminder of you. When the person takes the object away, they will not only take a reminder of the peaceful mind state, but also a symbol of your support, which they can keep with them between your meetings.

There is no need to be overly afraid of such connections, though we should be wary of encouraging people to become over-dependant on us. It is natural for people to develop feelings towards the person who is helping them. We can accept it as part of the relationship. For those whom we help, we are ourselves very significant objects.

EXERCISE FOUR: CREATING AN ANCHOR
(twenty minutes)

Find a small stone or similar object, which you can use to create an anchor for yourself to carry the feelings of calm which you develop in meditation. The stone should be small enough to slip into your pocket, so that you can carry this link around with you.

First take five minutes to ground yourself. You can do this in a sitting position. Be aware of your contact with the floor or chair. Feel yourself letting go into the support which the ground offers. Imagine your breath flowing down into the ground, anchoring you into the earth. Relax and allow the space between your shoulders to extend. Feel the air surrounding you and the flow of your breath through your body.

When you have settled yourself, bring your attention to the object which you have chosen. Hold it in your hand and feel its solidity. Use your fingers to explore its surface and examine its texture.

As you hold your object, breath deeply and evenly, imagining the breath flowing into your hands and, through them, into your object. Choose a word which you would like to build association with, such as *peace* or *calm*, and repeat the word to yourself with each breath. Keep breathing gently and repeating your word for about fifteen minutes.

When you are ready, bring your meditation to a close, hold

the object gently but more firmly than before, and feel its energy in your hand. Open your eyes and look at it, then place it in your quiet space where you can see it. Stretch and stand up in your own time.

Repeat this meditation every day for the coming week. You can either leave the object in the quiet space in between your meditations, or you can carry it with you in your pocket as a reminder of the calm you have created.

People as Objects

When people talk about their lives, they often talk about other people who are or have been significant to them. Encouraging a person to talk more about the significant people in their life can be very helpful.

The people in our lives have a strong influence and we often feel them to be with us even when they are not. We find ourselves thinking "John would say yes to that idea" or "Father wouldn't approve of that". Sometimes we look to our friends and relatives in our imagination for guidance. Faced with difficult situations we might think about how someone else would handle things. Feeling criticised, we might recall a person who has previously been judgemental of us. Feeling lonely, we might think of someone we love, comforting us. Children often have invisible friends, but adults too carry round bands of invisible others.

So when a person talks about friends or family, the people they mention may evoke strong reactions in them. We could say that they have a powerful conditioning effect on their mind. You will notice how, sometimes, this is positive and supportive, but other times it can be limiting or even frightening. In the extreme, someone may still feel terror, and have a sense of being in the presence of a person who abused them, even many decades later, when they talk about that person or remember them.

Of course, such relationships exist in the mind and may or may not accurately reflect the relationship with the real person. The images of people which we carry round may be out of date or distorted by our emotional responses to them or by our hopes or fears relating to them. Our relationships, especially with people whom we are close to, are complicated.

When someone talks about significant people, sometimes we may simply notice and appreciate the importance which that relationship has in the life of the person we are helping. We may encourage them to draw on the strength which the imagined presence gives them.

Other times, however, we may be conscious that the imagined relationship is not helpful and that expectations are unrealistic and perhaps getting in the way. If this is the case, you might find it helpful to gently prompt the person to look at the relationship more closely and encourage them to investigate the reality of it. Such investigations help a person let go of old perceptions and look in new ways. The aim is to help the speaker to see what is really true about the other, as opposed to what their own mind has created.

- You might ask things like:
- What sort of thing might they say in such and such a situation?
- What does he/she think when he/she sees you?
- What is he/she proud of?

Or even

- What sort of experiences did he/she have in childhood?
- What sort of thing does he/she like to wear, eat, read etc?

We will return to the question of significant others and ways of drawing out conversation about them in sessions seven and eight.

EXERCISE FIVE: PERSONAL MEANING AND OBJECTIVE REALITY

(fifteen minutes)

Take a large sheet of paper and divide it into two with a horizontal line. Think of a person who is important to you and write their name along the line.

Now think of all the things that person means to you, the things they give you, the things you admire in them, the things they say and do which impress you or which you think of as typical of them. Write words and phrases in the top half of your page to convey these things. Add anything that describes what this person means to you.

When the top half of the page is full, turn the paper the other way up so that the blank section is at the top of the page and the section in which you have been writing is at the bottom (your writing will be upside down).

Now use the questions in the last section to investigate the reality of this person. What sort of thing do they like? What do they wear? What do they believe? What experiences are significant for them? And so on. Try to think of them from their point of view rather than from your own.

When you have finished, reflect on the differences between the two halves of the page; your personal view of the person and the reality of the person, as far as you can ascertain it.

Focusing on Objects in a Story

As a person tells their story an array of objects is paraded before the listener. It is as if the person who is speaking is running a film in his or her mind on which different characters appear. When someone is really caught up in describing a significant event, and their whole attention is caught up with the scene they are describing, their emotions flow freely. Sometimes an emotion will be remembered in retrospect, but this itself becomes a object to which the person responds with new feelings.

A skill which counsellors, and others who work in psychological fields develop, is that of noticing which parts of the story and which objects are most significant. As you continue to listen to people you will find yourself sensing what the person needs to talk about and be able to help them to focus on the most important aspects of what they are saying. This is often done simply by using a reflective response which draws attention to the key point.

Often this involves naming the object that has just been referred to, as the following examples demonstrate:

- So your mother moved out at that point
- You lived in a caravan then
- The letter had a foreign stamp on it

Because our minds are conditioned by objects, drawing attention to the objects in this way is often more helpful than drawing attention to the feeling. If you highlight the significant object, the person will tell you about their feeling response, or more likely simply express the feeling. If you keep your responses factual and focused on the significant things in the story, this will give the person space to explore their experience without imposing your agenda or framework. The interaction will flow with the person's spontaneous process.

EXERCISE SIX: OBJECT FOCUSED RESPONSES
(twenty minutes)

Ahmed says: "My mother is in Pakistan and I haven't been able to contact her since there was trouble in the village."

Look at the following possible responses. Which ones focus on objects?

- You sound worried
- Tell me more about your mother
- Is the rest of your family in Pakistan?
- There was trouble?
- As you are talking, I imagine your mother at home in that small, rural community
- How does that make you feel?

Any of these responses are possible, but they will have different effects. Imagine being Ahmed and hearing each of them. What effect do you think each response is likely to have?

Make notes of your responses. Think of three other things which a listener might say. What would you say?

Placing emphasis on making reflections about objects rather than feelings is characteristic of the approach we are introducing here. Many popular therapy methods draw the person's attention towards their feelings, but this is often counter-productive.

As a person experiences the relationships and people and things of their world more vividly, they will flow with their emotions in a more natural and healthy way without the self-preoccupation which introspection can bring.

EXERCISE SEVEN: FINDING THE ENERGY
(twenty minutes)

Find a radio or television programme in which a person is telling a story. (Use a different one from ones you have used before.) Ideally the story should be about ten to fifteen minutes long.

Listen to the piece with a pad of paper in front of you. As you listen, note down the 'objects' that you hear in the story. (You do not need to get too caught up in deciding what an object is or including every small reference.)

As you go along, draw circles round each object, varying in size, depending on the relative significance each has.

Notice how the objects relate to one another. Some may be part of a group or almost inter-changeable. You will probably find that there are only a few really significant objects or clusters of objects.

Play the recording again and listen to the voice tone of the speaker. Do you notice any variations as they talk about the different objects? Does your assessment of what is significant change as your hear it a second time?

Offering Containment

Talking about objects which are significant to us can sometimes be surprisingly emotional. Allowing someone to cry and express grief or regret can be very healthy and being able to sit with someone who is crying can be the most important thing a listener does. Sometimes, however, you may feel someone is becoming too distressed and is feeling overwhelmed by emotion. You may feel that it is a good idea to help them to create some distance from the things that they have been talking about, at least for the present time.

Feelings such as grief are often best expressed in waves, with periods of intense weeping or unhappiness interspersed with more ordinary activity. Sometimes, too, the space in which you are talking feels too public and the person feels exposed and uncomfortable about expressing emotions. Other times you may need to finish talking for practical reasons. A session has come to an end and it is time to lock up the building and go home. Occasionally the person is becoming so overwhelmed by emotion that you are worried about their mental state. They may be becoming confused, or you may even worry about their ability to drive home.

For whatever reason, it can be useful to have some skills in helping a person to create more distance from the emotive material. You can do this by bringing them back to the ordinary things in the present moment. This is a kind of grounding exercise. To be effective, offering containment needs to be by way of practical instructions, and you may need to be quite directive.

Things which you might try are:

- Telling the person that it is time to put feelings aside, but that they can be returned to later.
- Asking about other things in a person's life
- Talking about mundane things
- Getting the person to tell you about things in the room which you are in – what do they like or dislike about the furnishings?
- Going for a cup of tea
- Going for a walk

If you do feel that you need to create this sort of closure in a conversation, be careful not to be too abrupt. It may be helpful to bring the person out of their emotional state at this point, but try to avoid giving the impression that the person has said the wrong thing. Make your suggestions gently but firmly and if appropriate tell the person why you are doing it.

For example you might say, "I'm aware we are going to have to be finishing for this week as we have to close the centre, and I can see you are still pretty shaken up by what you have been saying. We can come back to it next week, but right now, I think we need to put it away. I wonder if we could spend a couple of minutes talking about something completely different so that you can do that."

Session Six

We are Not Alone

This session will include:

- Community and support
- Exploring your own support systems
- Why support systems are important to people who care for others
- Looking at boundaries in helping relationships
- Pitfalls of breaking boundaries or seeking support inappropriately
- Spiritual friendship
- Helping people we work with to develop their support systems

A key factor in a person's psychological well being is their ability to step out of their personal viewpoint and see other people as having their own interests, responses and life paths. Spending time with other people and sharing conversation and leisure is important in creating the conditions for this to happen. If people are isolated, they retreat into their own world and get lost in rumination. Their mental health may well deteriorate in such circumstances. In community with others, they are naturally drawn out of their preoccupations and engage with other people and with life.

Many situations in which people offer befriending or listening services are in settings which are designed to offer not just one to one care, but a caring environment for people in crisis. People with mental health problems or people with specific troubles find refuge in groups with others who have similar difficulties. Whatever the situation, though, finding a listening ear is valuable, not just because of the quality of the listening which is provided or the advice given, but also because the listener offers human to human contact. The relationship with the listener, or with others in the same boat, breaks through the isolation which personal problems can bring and opens up new opportunities for sharing human interaction.

SUPPORT AND COMMUNITY

One of the things which many befriending and support agencies offer is a sense of community. Community is something which has been lost from big areas of modern society. Most people no longer live in the kind of close-knit relationships which people have lived in in the past. In many areas of the country there are no longer neighbours whose doors are open to us when things go wrong. We no longer know the people who sit beside us on the bus or train. Instead, we go about our lives treating others in functional ways and being wary of strangers.

This is not a healthy situation. Mental health depends upon our embeddedness in a community. So, for many people who you help, providing a friendly, supportive relationship may well be the most important thing you do.

EXERCISE ONE: REFLECTING ON COMMUNITY
(ten minutes)

Reflect on your experience of community. What do you understand by the term community? Has your own sense of community changed over your lifetime? What community or communities do you feel that you belong to now?

Reflect on the situation of people who you are helping or intend to help. What is their experience of community? Will your involvement with them change that sense of community? If so, how?

COMMUNITY AND CULTURE

Different cultures have their own views of community. Many people coming to the West as refugees or immigrants come from communities which have been tightly knit and supportive. It can be a shock to discover the level of individualism in the West and the lack of support from neighbours and acquaintances.

At the same time, people may be fleeing oppressive situations or extremes of poverty and deprivation. Even the poorest conditions in Britain or the US may seem luxurious by comparison with what has been left behind. Yet even in such circumstances, the difficulties of finding a supportive, warm reception can make arrival here a mixed blessing.

Different communities have different styles of operating. Working within communities to help them to establish their own support networks *in their own way* can be vital, since those communities may not readily take to Western models and ideals. We do better to take into account a diversity of views and look at what actually works for people, rather than following what the latest fashion in community development dictates.

Identifying the informal support structures that are already working is not always easy, however. Our expectations are conditioned by our prior experience and we may have all sorts of prejudices about what should be going on. These may prevent us from even seeing what is really there. In such situations it is a great privilege to be able to listen in depth to people, because the listening slows us down, and questions our assumptions, so that we gain insight into their world. We come to appreciate what is happening there in its own terms.

On the other hand, such appreciation should not prevent us from seeing the levels of suffering that may be involved in having been uprooted from one's home community or from seeing the oppression which exists for some groups within other cultures.

It is possible to be too rosy-eyed in our view. For some people there is no hidden network, and home culture may be punitive or abusive. We cannot generalise but need to listen to each person's story with an open mind and heart.

EXERCISE TWO: EXPLORING CULTURAL FACTORS IN COMMUNITY
(forty minutes)

Collect together a pile of magazines and newspapers. Cut out pictures from them that suggest community to you. Make a collage showing different aspects of community. When you have finished look at the image you have created.

Now think of what it is like to be someone of a different culture. You might think of someone from overseas, from a different walk of life, or of a different age. Think of a real person, perhaps one of the people you are working with, if this seems helpful.

Imagine yourself in the other person's shoes. Imagine being given the same task of making a collage of your view of community (as that person.)

Take a second piece of paper and on it create a second collage depicting their view of community.

Put the two images in front of you and reflect on the similarities and differences between them for five minutes.

So community can be a great source of support, or it can be a source of oppression. Depending on the particular values and ethos, and the place which a person occupies within the community, the experience may be very different.

One aspect of the listener's role is often to help to facilitate positive experiences of community, whether by supporting and building on what is already present, or by creating new settings in which community can emerge. Community based projects clearly have this sort of function, but most agencies can have some aspect of this kind.

Helping Others to Find Community

Many groups that offer listening and support effectively create community for the people who use them. This can happen in practical ways, through shared activities, outings and support in the house, or it can happen by building relationships, through encouraging people to meet in groups or to share the use of facilities.

As we have seen, mental health depends on engaging with others. Community activities can, therefore, be very valuable in creating healthy environments for people who might otherwise sink into isolation and the sort of miserable self-preoccupation which may follow it. Skilful use of activities can encourage people to engage with one another, seeing each other as real people with real feelings and preferences. In this way, many of the things which we have discussed in previous sessions naturally occur.

Activity helps people to find comfortable ways of interacting with one another. It is possible to relate to others on different levels when you are involved in a group doing practical things. Sometimes it is good to work alongside others in silence or to do a task on your own, knowing that others are in the next room. Other times it is good to talk. Practical activity offers variety and allows people to naturally find their own levels.

Besides encouraging people to relate to others, these sorts of activities also bring people into contact with physical work and physical objects. This can be very grounding. Cooking, cleaning, gardening and other tasks can be healing for people who are stressed or cut off from their feelings. They literally bring people 'out of themselves', into contact with the real world, and with objects. The practical focus of such tasks is coupled with the opportunity to work alongside other people. This combination encourages engagement on both physical and social levels and so may provide some of the healthiest ways of offering support.

Supporting the Listener

If you are working as a listener, it is important to have your own support system. Many projects that offer befriending, or listening services provide their volunteers or staff with support. This support, when it is formal, is usually called *supervision*.

Supervision is intended to give you a place where you can discuss your work and get feedback. It means that you are not working in isolation so that if things feel difficult in a helping relationship, or you have a dilemma about how to respond to someone, you have somewhere to turn. It also means that you can discuss your role and become clearer about the scope of what you are doing, and where the line is between personal and work-related matters.

Good supervision gives you:
• Someone to talk your work through with
• Someone who can help you decide what is the best approach to specific people or eventualities
• A place to review your work and reflect on ways of improving it, future training needs, and so on
• An opportunity to talk about personal feelings which have been raised by the work so that you do not risk burdening the people you are helping
• Somewhere to check out your hunches
• Someone who can advise you when you may be getting out of

your depth
- Sometimes supervision happens in a group, and then you may learn from hearing other more experienced listeners talking about their work

---

EXERCISE THREE: REVIEWING SUPERVISION
(five minutes)

- What sort of supervision arrangements do you have for your work?
- Are there things which you would like to change about them?
- What do you get from supervision?
- Could you use it better?

Make notes and if you feel you need to make changes, discuss them with whoever manages the situation in which you work.

Getting Support from the Right Place

Being a listener can be quite a complicated business. Counsellors work in situations where there are tight boundaries and it is very clear what should and should not be talked about with clients. They have professional codes and guidelines and are required to work with regular supervision.

Listening and befriending relationships are much more complicated because they often do not have such tight rules and guidelines. Projects and agencies where listening happens vary greatly. Sometimes you may have good supervision from someone who is experienced in the field, but in other helping roles this may not be available. Some people who are doing listening and befriending work in teams and have a good peer support network, others may be isolated, working things out on their own by trial and error.

EXERCISE FOUR: YOUR SUPPORT NETWORK
(twenty minutes)

Draw a diagram to show your personal support network. Mark yourself with a small circle and then mark in all the people to whom you turn when you need support. You may like to use different sized circles to represent the different quantities of support which different people offer, and you could use different colours to show the different types of difficulty you might take to different people.

Think about whom you might turn to with the following:
- Feeling lonely
- Anxiety about your health
- The car has broken down
- You have had a big gas bill which you can't afford
- You need a baby sitter

(add some examples of your own.)

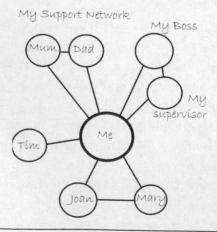

Whilst supervision and professional support varies for people working in less formal or community-based settings, listeners in such settings are often put into quite complicated situations, where it may be difficult to maintain clear boundaries. People working in community-based roles may be meeting with the people whom they are supporting in a more social environment, where conversation and behaviour seems more relaxed and casual. They may meet with service users for less defined lengths of time, sometimes being around each other all day, as in a day-centre or drop-in setting. It may be more difficult and less appropriate to keep tight limits on what you share in such circumstances.

In addition, the people you are supporting in such settings may see more of your life than a counsellor's clients would. They are probably interested in you as a person and may ask questions out of ordinary chattiness. Refusing to say anything can seem standoffish and unnecessary. In such circumstances, it may be good for you to share some things about your personal life, but deciding what is all right to share and what may be inappropriate can be difficult.

These problems are not easily solved, and gaining the ability to manage the different relationships and set appropriate limits often comes through bitter experience. Discussion with colleagues and supervisors can help. So too can a view of what you are trying to achieve in the helping relationship. What you do or say should be in the interests of the people you are helping, and not about meeting your personal needs. There are many considerations, however.

One obvious consideration is about not burdening the people whom you are helping by telling them about your own troubles or concerns. If you are in a helping role, it is not appropriate to look for support from the people you are helping. If you need help or support it is important to find it from friends or go to a counsellor.

If you do tell people about things in your personal life, for any reason, you need to think through the impact it will have on them. One rule of thumb which you might use is that you should only share something if it will be helpful to the other person in some way. The difficulty with this suggestion, however, is that people often think that, because they have solved a particular problem in their own lives, they can give advice to others in the same situation.

If you think this, be careful. It is generally a fallacy. Although you may have a greater appreciation of the dilemmas someone in a similar situation might be facing, you probably don't have the answer which they need. They have to find the answer for themselves.

A third consideration is that by sharing personal information, you change the relationship you have with the person. If you tell a person something about yourself, this will alter their view of you. For example, even something as simple as telling them that you are married may affect how they see you. Their image of a married person may be completely different from that of a single person, and this will colour how they see you. Depending on their own circumstances they may envy you, identify with you, be attracted to you or feel sorry for you.

If you tell people about your children, your recent bereavement, your home life, it will change their view of you and may make some things difficult to talk about. On the other hand, sometimes it can be helpful. One person may feel more able to confide their anxieties about their children if they know you are a parent, but someone else may be put off talking about their recent abortion if they know that you have children. There are always pros and cons, and sometimes these are not immediately apparent.

Each case needs to be thought through.

EXERCISE FIVE: CONSEQUENCES OF PERSONAL SHARING

(ten minutes)

A volunteer at a community centre receives a phone call at work from her boyfriend. He tells her that he has just come off his motor bike and has been taken to the casualty department at the local hospital, where he is waiting for an x-ray on his arm, which seems to be broken.

At the time there are two groups using the centre, a drop-in support group for young single mothers and a lunch club for elderly people.

What sort of complications might there be in the following responses:
- If the volunteer shares her anxieties with young people using the drop-in?
- If she talks with people in the lunch club?
- If she decides to leave work and go to the hospital to support her boyfriend?
- If she leaves but does not explain why?
- If she does not leave but waits till after work to check up on how her boyfriend is doing.

When you are supporting others, it is important that you try to keep the helping relationship clean of personal agendas from your side. This does not mean that you have to act as an automaton and cannot show your human side. Sometimes a worker's personal crisis can be very helpful in taking a helping relationship to new depths. Basically, though, you are not in it to get your needs met. Nor are you there to convert someone to your religion, to find a sexual partner or a friend, to get someone to fix your drains or to get involved in financial deals.

Boundaries in Listening Relationships

As we have already seen, there are many potential complications in relationships with people we are helping. Whilst we may be befriending a person, we do not generally become their friend in the commonly used meaning of the term. This can lead to misunderstandings. Sometimes the person we are helping wants us to be friends. They may be lonely and see the listener as someone they could enjoy seeing more of. They may idealise the listener and imagine them as a perfect confidante, always available and sympathetic, or the source of wise advice. They might be attracted to the listener and fantasise about a romantic relationship.

When people are vulnerable and lonely, such reactions are not really surprising, especially when the listener is someone who seems to be so kind and competent.

EXERCISE SIX: EXPLORING BOUNDARIES IN YOUR WORK
(fifteen minutes)

Which of these activities do you think are unsuitable for a listener or befriender to do with someone whom they are supporting? Are there some circumstances where they would be okay and others where they would not?

- Asking a service user to help repair your car
- Going to the cinema together
- Meeting for coffee away from the centre where you normally meet
- Inviting a service user to your wedding

- Visiting a service user in hospital
- Giving a home phone number to a service user
- Telling a service user about your forthcoming operation
- Asking a service user to do the washing up
- Telling a service user why another regular user has not come this week
- Inviting a service user to your home
- Bringing your children to the project or centre where you work

Identify the scenarios which you feel are tricky from this point of view. What do you think might be the consequence of doing some of the things you have labelled as unhelpful?

There are not necessarily fixed answers to these questions. Because of the variety of settings in which listening skills are used, it is not possible to generalise, but it is important to think about the possible consequences of getting involved with service users in these kinds of situations before you get out of your depth. If you are involved in listening in an agency, discuss your responses with others in that agency. Raise any queries with your supervisor if you have one or with whoever manages your agency.

If you give in to requests to meet the ideals and fantasies which other people hold of you, you are likely to find all sorts of problems follow. Many people in helping professions have, for the best intentions (or sometimes not such good ones) fallen into situations where they have tried to have these sorts of relationships with people they were supposed to be helping and have come badly unstuck. For this reason, professions which care for people such as counsellors, doctors, teachers, clergy, social workers and so on have all developed strict codes of behaviour which define boundaries which the people in that profession should not overstep.

EXERCISE SEVEN: DIFFERENT RELATIONSHIPS, DIFFERENT BOUNDARIES
(fifteen minutes)

Think about times when you or a close friend has sought support from someone. Try to make a list of ten different scenarios, some in formal settings and others in less formal settings.

Think about the type of relationship which you or your friend had with the person who gave the support.

In each case, what sort of qualities did the relationship have which made it possible to get support? What sort of boundaries operated in each scenario? (Even in ordinary friendships there will no doubt have been some limits.)

Did the boundaries help the situation, or did they cause problems?

A boundary is an invisible line. It may be marked in some way, perhaps by a fence or wall, but basically it is a demarcation of space. Professional boundaries are lines which distinguish between acceptable behaviour and problematic behaviour, and that demarcate personal space which is not to be intruded upon.

Since this book is intended for people in a wide variety of situations which vary in their particular interpretations of ethical boundaries I cannot offer absolute guidance on boundaries in your agency, but we can look broadly at the types of area which might be considered problematic and at some of the broad issues involved. From these you can reflect on your own agency's guidelines and raise questions or concerns with those who formulate them if necessary.

AVAILABILITY

As a listener, you will probably have to think about how you manage your time and how far you make yourself available to different people. This might include thinking about how often you spend time with any particular person, what sort of time you give. (Do you give them undivided attention or do you spend time with them in a more informal setting, say in a drop-in, where you are also giving attention to other people.)

There are two things to take into account. Firstly, you need to consider what your priorities are. How much time can you spend in intensive listening, and how much needs to be spent on other activities? Who is most needy of that time and how will you share it out? If you simply respond to demands as they arise you will soon find your time being taken up by the people with the most persistent voices, who will not necessarily be those with the greatest need.

Secondly, you need to think about the best interests of the person whom you are listening to. These interests may include having some limits set. Without such limits, those who dominated your time would be likely to talk in an unfocused way rather than valuing your attention. Setting some limits, perhaps by giving quality time to the person once or twice a week and keeping other conversations functional and brief, would make the person more likely to use their time with you well. Setting limits can also be an education for some people. Their best interests may include learning to appreciate that other people have needs too and that you, as their supporter, are not universally available.

Although it may seem tough, such encounters with reality, when sensitively handled, can help a person become more realistic in their expectations and more mature in their relationships.

Agencies which offer more formal listening or counselling usually have their own policies on the availability of staff. These might involve limits on times when the person is available, on where they can be seen, and on how long they can give to the person seeking help. In some situations there might be appointment systems or ways of making referrals. Counselling agencies often have a policy about the sort of availability a listener might offer, whether it is an hour long session once a week, or limited to six sessions in total.

In informal settings, it can be more difficult to regulate time spent with individuals, and the listener may sometimes have to create their own limits in specific instances. For example, if you are working in a community based drop-in which is used by people with mental health or social problems, you may well find that many of the users would like to talk with you at length every day about their difficulties. This is problematic. Giving such a level of attention to one or two people would prevent you from carrying out other aspects of your work.

Similarly, you may need to limit the length of your conversations. In most listening settings it is only rarely appropriate to continue working with one person for more than an hour, and in many instances shorter times are normal. Occasionally, there may be exceptions. It is important that the length of time which you give to someone is a function of what is useful and what you are able to offer, rather than being determined by your anxiety about ending the session.

Ending a conversation can be particularly hard if the service user comes to visit you in a space which normally has no boundaries. Professionals in such situations learn skills in ending interactions once they have ceased to be useful. For example, the priest is likely to become adept at gently ushering talkative parishioners towards the door after they have been listening for a suitable time.

This latter situation raises the question of what boundary exists between work and home. In most settings the listener is not working from home. In such situations the listener would be unlikely to give out a home phone number or address to a service user. There are, however, exceptions, such as that of clergy or people who are running some types of support group, where it would be quite appropriate to give out personal contact information. If you are in such a situation you may need to learn to be assertive in managing your time.

EXERCISE EIGHT: AVAILABILITY
(five minutes)

If you are involved in a listening role, think about the question of availability. If someone wants to talk to you, how do they get to do so? What sorts of things are possible? Where do you meet them? What is not acceptable to you or to the agency? Have you ever had dilemmas about the limits you set?

RELATIONSHIPS

We have already discussed some of the issues which are involved in personal sharing. Whilst in many situations some personal sharing is quite helpful, knowing where to draw the line can be difficult. As a general rule, the guideline that *any sharing should be for the benefit of the service user and not yourself* is a good test, but the answer may not always be clear cut.

An area that is more clear cut is that of romantic or sexual involvement. It is virtually never acceptable for someone in the role of listener to become involved with someone they are supporting in this way. Unfortunately, it is quite common for people who are vulnerable to be attracted to the person who is supporting them. Other people, particularly if they have had bad experiences in the past, may be very sensitive to anything which could be read as a sexual overture, even where none was intended. It follows from this that one needs to be wary of doing things which might give false hope or the wrong messages.

Things to be wary of might include:

- Giving personal details to the person
- Any breach of normal boundaries, such as meeting up privately outside the agency
- Meeting in places that might be seen as romantic like a coffee shop or restaurant
- Going into a person's bedroom
- Touch of any kind
- Giving or receiving gifts
- Accepting an invitation from the person
- Comforting and reassuring the person when they are distressed
- Flirtatious or coy mannerisms
- Anything which you feel embarrassed to share with your supervisor or line manager

The difficulty is that one can think of scenarios where some of these things might be part of the normal work of someone in a listening or supporting role. Where this is the case, there is probably no problem, but the important thing is to be aware of what might be read into the behaviour and be careful not to inadvertently act seductively.

EXERCISE NINE: PROBLEMS OF SEXUAL ATTRACTION

(five minutes)

Have you ever been in a situation where someone was attracted to you, but you were not attracted to them? How did you handle the situation?

How might you handle a similar situation if the person who was attracted to you were someone you were supporting in your role as a listener?

CONFIDENTIALITY

Most agencies have policies on confidentiality. These usually balance the service user's right to tell you things, without fear of it being passed on to others, against various concerns about safety of the person sharing the information or of third parties.

Appropriate professional sharing of personal information about users is usually of two kinds.

Some information sharing is intended to benefit the user. This might involve different people conferring to decide on what is the best way forward in helping the person. It might include discussing treatment plans or social programmes.

Some information sharing is intended to benefit third parties or to protect the user. In particular, this might include protection of children or vulnerable adults, or protecting people who are suicidal or otherwise a danger to themselves.

Another place where it is appropriate to talk about things which people have told you is in supervision. If you have supervision, you will talk about the conversations you have had. This discussion should be respectful and in many cases need not include details which could identify the person you are talking about. You need not give the person's name.

In small agencies, however, the identities of people being discussed may be very obvious, and there may be staff discussion of how to handle situations which are arising. These may well involve sharing otherwise confidential information. Supervision may be done by senior staff members who are working in the same situation, who have also seen incidents or heard accounts of them, and the supervisor may well have views about what ought to be done, which they have arrived at independently of what the listener is sharing. Such situations are complex and require sensitive handling.

Other sharing of information which occurs in some agencies is not helpful at all. In some settings staff may tend to gossip about users. Policies about confidentiality are clear in some agencies, but in others, expectations may be less so. Even where there are policies, interpretation may vary, and, unless the issue of confidentiality is reviewed periodically, there can be slippage where people become careless in their conversations.

EXERCISE TEN: LIMITS TO CONFIDENTIALITY
(five minutes)

When someone confides in you in your role of listener, who might you talk to about what they had said? Why might you discuss it? How might you discuss it?

SAFEGUARDING CHILDREN AND PROTECTION OF VULNERABLE ADULTS

Agencies have responsibilities to report instances of child abuse. If you suspect that a child or young person is being abused, you need to seek guidance from a supervisor or manager immediately. Similar policies are usually in place in relation to vulnerable adults, such as the elderly or those with learning difficulties. Volunteers in the UK are now usually required to have CRB (Criminal Records Bureau) checks which will investigate any history of relevant convictions.

This said, there are still grey areas and problems which arise from such policies. For example, many agencies have a policy of warning young people that if they disclose abuse, the agency will have to report it. This can cause difficulties as it can leave the young person, who does not want the services to intervene, with no one to talk to.

FINANCE

As a powerfully symbolic commodity, money can cause all sorts of complications in support relationships. A useful guideline is not to get involved financially with someone with whom you have a listening role. This generally means not getting involved in:

- Shared business ventures
- Borrowing or lending money
- Employing a person who is currently a service user
- Accepting money other than an agreed payment or donation to the agency

Of course, once again, there may be all kinds of exceptions. In some agencies, users may do work for the agency or donate money to it. Some institutions, such as churches or charities, rely on donations from people who attend their meetings. Although this does not usually go to the listener personally, sometimes the distinction between the listener and the agency may not be very clear, especially in the mind of the person offering the money or time. It is wise to be wary of large donations from service users or of complicated financial or work-related arrangements with them. Though not always problematic in practice, such arrangements are usually best made at the policy level with a number of people involved in the decision.

RECORD KEEPING

Any records which are kept by agencies should be treated with great care. They should be confidential, and should remain in a locked cupboard or similar place. Most records are now, in theory at least, available for consultation by the person who they refer to. They may also, in extreme situations, be brought into legal investigations. All this has led those in helping professions to become extremely wary of what they write about service users or clients in official records. The main guidance is to stick to facts and to keep the record minimal.

If records are kept in your agency, discuss what should or should not be written down with your manager or supervisor. If necessary, take advice from people in similar organisations. If you ever keep personal notes on a user, treat them with great care and destroy them as soon as possible. Do not include anything which might lead a third party to identify the person if they accidentally found your notes. If you are ever involved in a legal request to release notes, take advice from a professional body before doing so.

ADVICE GIVING

Some listeners give advice, others do not. Only give advice if it is clearly within your agency policy for you to do so. If you give advice, be clear that it is:

- Within the remit of what you are expected to do
- Impartial
- Accurate
- Appropriate to the person to whom it is given
- Clear and unambiguous

Spiritual Friendship

There is a concept which is found in various religious traditions which is called *spiritual friendship*. A spiritual friend is someone who has your best interests at heart rather than someone who will indulge your latest whim. This means that the person who is a good spiritual friend will do things that support you in becoming more spiritually mature rather than just in doing things you find pleasurable or distracting.

The notion of spiritual friendship is a useful one for the befriender. A spiritual friend should not be looking out for personal advantage or pleasure. You can trust a spiritual friend not to have hidden agendas. A spiritual friend may be challenging, and not accept our excuses. He or she will expect the best of us, and gently (or not so gently) encourage us to come up with it.

The spiritual friend is someone who naturally keeps the sorts of boundaries which we have been discussing in this session. Of course, many of us would hope to offer friendship of this type to all our friends, but, being human, we often fall short and are concerned with our own needs. Becoming a listener is one way of practising being a spiritual friend in a limited, and so perhaps manageable, situation. Guidelines and boundaries can help us to recognise when our own needs are starting to spill over into the helping relationship and we have stopped having our focus on the user's well being.

REFLECTION
Sit in your quiet space and bring your attention to your breathing.

After a few minutes, bring to mind the setting in which you

---

are offering listening care to others. Recall the place or places in which you work and specific people with whom you work.

In your mind, gradually bring together an assembly of people to whom you offer care. Try to hold them in a peaceful place in your heart.

Now, as you hold them in your attention, think:
May these people be safe.
May these people be free from harm.
May I act in ways which support their well being.
May I not act in ways which threaten it.

Repeat these wishes to yourself and, as you do so, visualise a light growing which holds both you and the people whom you are helping.

When the light has grown to full brightness, enjoy your remaining reflection time in silence.

Session Seven

Relationships and Connections

This session will include:

- Expectations and conditioned relationships
- Scripts and storylines
- The ways that our thinking is conditioned by our views of others
- Significant relationships and their impact
- Inspirational figures
- Biographical and family history work

We have already seen how important stories are to people's mental states. The ideas which we have about life are often framed in the accounts which we give to ourselves of events from the past and stories which we tell ourselves about what is going on in the present. These stories shape the way that we behave, since we tend to act according to the storyline which is implicit in our thinking. It is as if we already know the script and the different parts which we have to act out. We simply find new stages on which to play it.

Expectations in Relationships

When we are acting in this way, playing out our personal storyline, we tend to draw others into the drama. Other people also have their parts to play. All of us have expectations about how the people around us will act. We anticipate that the people we encounter will behave in ways which are predicted by our stories. If we have experienced a lot of criticism, we expect others whom we meet to be critical. If we have experienced people in authority as being untrustworthy, we are likely to be suspicious of anyone who has power to make decisions which affect us. Sometimes the storyline which we play out involves a person who never actually existed, perhaps someone we longed for because we felt something was missing in our lives. For example, if we have fantasies of having someone to love us completely, we may well go through life looking for the perfect partner or for mother figures who will care for us.

EXERCISE ONE: IDENTIFYING REPEATING PATTERNS
(ten minutes)

Think about your own relationships. Are there common trends in them? Do you keep being attracted to similar people, or play out similar scenarios with friends? Do you have repeating patterns of arguments? Do you repeatedly hope for certain responses and find yourself disappointed over and over again?

Think back over a number of significant friendships or a number of romantic involvements which you have had and see whether you can identify any such patterns. You can use a timeline diagram to explore these patterns and similarities if you want to take this further.

If you do identify patterns, what do you think they might be about? Are they repeating some early storyline or an expectation or hope which you are carrying?

What effect do you think these patterns have on your behaviour and on the people whom you are relating to?

Expectations and distortions are so much part of our normal way of seeing the world that we hardly notice them. We just assume our assessments of people are accurate. We don't question our own assumptions. Conversely, the other people involved may well not be aware that we are holding all sorts of false expectations and impressions of them. They have their own set of expectations. Sometimes these mesh well with ours. Although we may in one sense miss one another, in another sense our relationship is a comfortable fit. Other times they differ and misunderstandings arise.

Although these hidden factors go on in all relationships, mostly we are not conscious of what we are acting out. This said, people are often partially aware of their patterns of responding to other people. It is quite common for people to say things like "I have real difficulties with women bosses," or "I'm always falling for father figures."

However, frequently these generalisations are not questioned. People often enjoy expounding their world view and identifying with it. They continue to say things like "young men are only into beer," or "foreign doctors are terribly patronising," even when, if they thought about it more seriously, they might think differently. Our stories may, thus, become the basis for prejudice. They simplify our lives by excluding sections of the population from real consideration.

Such attitudes often flow from cultural stereotypes and are held by groups which we belong to, rather than being ideas we created personally. Groups often use such prejudices to support collective identities, differentiating themselves from other groups by labelling them as different or inferior or by adopting different modes of thinking or doing things.

EXERCISE TWO: STORIES AND STEREOTYPES
(fifteen minutes)

This exercise is designed to help you identify stories and stereotyped responses which you are familiar with. In order to do it, you will need to take the following list and, if possible, ask someone else to read it out to you fairly quickly, pausing after each category of people so that you can write down your immediate response. Write quickly so that you do not have time to deliberate. Try to avoid thinking about the task or being 'politically correct' in your answers. Only you need to see what you write. The intention is to uncover some the hidden stories which you may be carrying, or those which you have picked up from others. These hidden stories are often stereotyped or prejudiced. Here is the list to read out:

Bus drivers
Old ladies
Americans
Dentists
Teenage girls
Head teachers
Footballers
Vicars
Counsellors
Bank managers
Immigrants
Dinner ladies
Estate agents
Consultants
Disabled people
Farm workers

Indian shopkeepers
Elderly gentlemen
Fashion models
Politicians

When you have finished, take time to look back over your responses. Which responses were strongest? Look at each response in turn and think about what that response might be based on?

Many are likely to be based on common culturally based stereotypes. Do others link to more personal stories? Do the stereotypes have personal resonances?

How do these stereotypes affect your responses when you meet real people who fit the categories?

Think about whether there are other categories of people whom you tend to have strong expectations of.

EXERCISE THREE: ROLES AND RELATIONSHIPS
(fifteen minutes)

Think of your family and friends and make a list of twenty people.

If you had to cast a play by matching your list of family and friends to the list of roles which you identified in exercise two above, whom would you assign to which part? Does your choice of people for roles throw any light on your prejudices or expectations about people you know?

We have already seen how the *objects* which we encounter condition our mental framework. Depending on what we are giving our attention to, our mood and thoughts may vary greatly. Many objects which take up our attention represent significant people in our lives. These objects may be the people themselves, people who remind us of other significant people, or they may be things which symbolise or are associated with significant people.

Whether we are talking about people or things, there are always at least two aspects to that person or thing. The object is:

- something that exists in its own right
- something which is seen as a whole set of associations.

When we meet a person, we have our picture of them, which may or may not be accurate. We may see them or we may see 'a mother figure' or 'a successful person'. The person also exists in their own reality, of which our view is only ever partial. (This is further complicated, of course, by the fact that the other person also has their own story about themselves, which may or may not be accurate.)

These two modes of seeing are also there in our memories of people whom we have known in the past. For example, I might remember my grandmother as a warm, cuddly person who told me stories and made everything alright for me, or I might realise that she was actually struggling to come to terms with her increasing ill health and with being widowed. I might look at her as I saw her when I was a child or I might reassess her life with new knowledge which I have gained as an adult.

These two aspects of our experience of others lead to two modes of exploration:

- We can talk about the person or object in terms of the way that we see them. This might involve finding out more about the story we are telling ourselves about them, its history and implications. It might mean changing the story so that we can find a new story which works better and gives us a more positive view of the person.

- We can investigate the reality of our perception and challenge our assumptions.

The advantage of exploring our perception of other people, as opposed to inanimate objects, is that, if we are still in contact with them, they are able to speak for themselves. If we are willing to listen, they are able to tell us how they do or do not fit our assumptions. Investigating the gap between assumptions and reality is, therefore, one important aspect of inter-personal work.

This kind of awareness is something which will arise naturally, both for ourselves and for those we work with, if we engage in meaningful conversation with them or if we invite them to speak to one another in settings where they are encouraged to go beyond habitual stereotypes. This is one of the advantages of working in community settings. People can be brought together with others whom they might have ignored on the street. In individual counselling, it is possible for a person to hold onto an artificial view of the counsellor. The counsellor may well appear like the sympathetic ideal whom the client has longed for as a parent or friend, or indeed may remain pretty invisible during the limited interaction of the session. In community settings the view, which a user has of others, is likely to be much more rounded.

Some of the methods in this session and the next will be about exploring our relationships with others, the ways that they impact on our thinking and attitudes. In particular we will look at ways of developing the kind of view of others that can allow us to see them with respect and not simply as bit-parts in our own lives. Some of these exercises will help you to investigate your own view, but you can also see how observation and engagement with others can help you and others to break out of stereotyped thought.

EXERCISE FOUR: LISTENING TO STORIES OF OTHERS
(indeterminate)

Take opportunities to have conversations with people about the significant people in their lives.

Notice how they talk about the people closest to them. How much do you think you are hearing about the real person? Would you recognise the significant person, if you met them?

What sorts of preoccupations and assumptions do you hear in the person's story? What do these say about the person who is speaking?

Significant Others

Some people are enormously influential in our lives. Many therapies emphasise our relationships with parents and other early relationships. Most of us can also think of a number of other important figures who have been significant in our early life, including teachers, neighbours, friends and other relatives.

Therapies which focus on early life tend to focus on the effect which these relationships have had on the client. Few spend time looking at what the person concerned was really like. The client's interests and story remain central and often the facts which are presented are left unquestioned. Therapists will say that they are not concerned with the objective truth of the matter, but, rather, with the client's experience. They may, thus, implicitly accept the version being presented as a truth, validating it, at least in the eyes of the client.

HABITUAL VIEWS

When we listen to someone who is telling us about their relative or friend, there is often an implicit invitation to validate the view which is being presented. This is not necessarily a bad thing.

Elsie talks at length about how her husband never speaks to her and spends most evenings at the pub. She wants the listener to understand her loneliness and frustration with him.

The person who confides in a befriender often does so because he wants someone to 'be on his side'. This search for support may well have roots in the person's lack of confidence or in negative stories which they are telling themselves.

On the other hand, people get stuck in habitual views and this becomes limiting. Some perspectives are negative and there may come a point when it is helpful to gently encourage the person to think in other ways, particularly if their story seems well rehearsed and intransigent. Looking afresh at early relationships, or at current ones, and seeing them in a new light can be very freeing.

Even when someone is stuck in a positive view of a significant person from their past, the effect may not be helpful. A person may talk endlessly about how wonderful a parent or mentor was until everyone who knows them is fed up with hearing the stories. Often those listening doubt whether the person really was as remarkable as the accounts suggest. They may be right. It may be that the positive view is repeated so vehemently because the person telling the story is actually trying to repress negative memories of the person they are describing. It may be that the person is idealising someone else and blaming them self as a way of holding onto a particular sense of identity or of avoiding having to make changes in their life.

EXERCISE FIVE: REPEATING STORIES OF RELATIONSHIP

(five minutes)

Think of a person that you know who tends to repeat the same stories about a relative, partner or other person. How do you respond?

Why do you think this person repeats the story? Is there an implicit message in the story? Why do they tell it to you? Do they tell it to other people? Are there ways that you could get beyond the story and encourage the person to talk about other aspects of the relationship or reassess it?

If you have the opportunity, try to follow this exercise up by talking to the person. Can you help the person to tell the story in a way that goes beyond their usual 'script'? This might mean going into more depth, or telling you about things which happened before or after the incident, or about other factors which they have not shared before. Try out your hunches about how you might arrive at a more direct conversation with the person.

APPRECIATING OUR CONNECTIONS

When we think about the impact of significant people in our lives, we may feel deeply moved. We may become aware of the origins of many of our feelings and reactions and attitudes and the way that these are tied into our history. We become aware of the others who have supported us throughout life.

The people who have been important in our lives over a period of time are our travelling companions. Family, old friends, or neighbours in settled communities may see each other grow through different life stages. As adults, they remember childhood events. As old people, they remember the times when families were young.

People often gain immense comfort from spending time in the company of people who have this longstanding view of them or from reconnecting with friends and acquaintances from childhood or early life. Reminiscing together validates the story of our lives and also sometimes helps us to find new meaning in the familiar, or to put painful memories into perspective, as new angles emerge. The old school reunion or a trip back to childhood haunts can be very powerful emotionally.

EXERCISE SIX: EXPLORING OLD THEMES
(five minutes)

Think about the last time that you met up with family or old friends and talked about the past.

What did you talk about? Did the conversation follow familiar tracks or did you discover new things? What effect did the conversation have on you?

BROKEN CONNECTIONS

For some people, such connections are not so easy to find. The elderly may see loved ones and friends die one by one until they are left isolated with no one to hold or reflect their memories. For them, photographs and mementos become very important as repositories for the life story. Taking an interest in them may bring alive a past which is slipping into oblivion.

Other people are alienated from the people who have been important in their lives or separated from them for one reason or another. Perhaps they have fallen out with family and friends or moved away and lost contact. Maybe the significant people in their lives have died or abandoned them. Perhaps they have moved country or are refugees and have had connections severed by war, violence or political conflict.

For people who have lost the everyday connections with people who share their stories and history, isolation can be awful. The listener's role in listening to the person's stories and offering the sort of validation which most people get from friends and family becomes very important. Sometimes the person who has time to sit and share the memories becomes a life-line.

EXERCISE SEVEN: EXPLORING ISOLATION
(five minutes)

Think of somebody you know who does not seem to have any close family or longstanding friends.

How do you think this person feels about their situation? Who do you think they look to for the sort of validation which others might find in family? How might you help a person in this position in your role as listener?

Inspiration

In session one, you looked at people who have been inspirational to you in your life. It may be that, as a listener, you will have a role in helping other people to find inspiring role models and to recognise the part that others have played in their lives.

In ordinary conversation, when they are talking about their lives, people frequently talk about those people who have been important to them. The person speaks with enthusiasm, their voice tone reflecting their admiration, and there is brightness in their eyes as they recount incidents involving the person who influenced them when they were young. Perhaps it was a teacher, maybe a member of the family, a grandparent or a family friend. They speak with wistfulness as they talk of what the person meant and how they wish they could have achieved as much or been as good.

Supporting such comments, and encouraging the person to tell you more of their story, may bring them into closer touch with the memories. It is good to be reminded of those who have been important to us. Partly, this is because we often feel a lot of gratitude to such people for what they gave us when we were younger. Also, by reconnecting with the memory, sometimes we are inspired afresh. We look back at the person's life through adult eyes and realise that, yes, this was an impressive person. We feel privileged to have known them.

When someone is inspired, they grow in capacity. They discover within themselves qualities which echo those of the person who has inspired them. For people who are struggling in life, recalling the strength of a family member who survived against the odds in the depression or the war or in some personal crisis, can give the impetus to carry on. The sense that this was *my* grandmother or *my* father creates identification, but the sense of their separate achievement also gives room for admiration. They can become role models.

EXERCISE EIGHT: EXPLORING ROLE MODELS
(five minutes)

Think about relatives or figures from your early life who have inspired you. What was it about each of them that inspired you? What stories or incidents do you recall about them? What influence have they had on your current life? How are you like each of them?

If you are working in group settings or with people who lack roots in their lives, or are facing particular difficulties, you might look for opportunities to introduce stories of people who might function as role models. Role models do not have to be historic figures or related to the person. Many of our role models are relatively ordinary people who we have met in the course of our adult lives and found interesting or inspiring.

For example, if you are running a support group, it can be inspiring to bring in a speaker who can talk about their own struggles with the particular problem which group members face, and how they have overcome or come to terms with it.

Sometimes, it may be helpful to introduce someone who will be challenging or may help people to think in new and creative ways, such as an artist or someone from a different cultural background. This should not, however, be done with any implication of telling the group how to deal with their problems, particularly if the person coming in appears to be of a different class or income group. A group might then, quite understandably, respond with a reaction of "it's all very well for them!"

If you are working with individuals, you may find it helps to talk about books or films which address their experience, as these can often be a source of ideas or inspiration. The popularity of autobiographical accounts of survivors of all manner of abuse or tragedies testifies to this. Whilst some readers are no doubt voyeuristic, many read such books because they offer a sense of community with fellow sufferers. The advantage of books or films is that they can be discussed in a more open way, without anyone feeling they have to take into account other people's sensibilities. People can say "well I wouldn't have done that!" or "Fancy carrying on like that!" without offending anyone.

Sometimes we are inspired by people who we have known. Other times we are inspired by strangers. We are inspired by different people for different reasons. Some people have lived exciting or dangerous lives and we admire their spiritedness.

Other people have been exemplary and are admired for their kindness and openheartedness. Some people we wish to emulate, whereas others we admire because they are so different from us.

MEDITATION ON AN INSPIRATIONAL PERSON
(twenty minutes)

Find a picture of someone whom you have found inspirational. It might be of someone you have known personally, or it might be somebody famous, either living or historic.

Sit in your quiet space and place the picture in front of you. Settle yourself by paying attention to your body resting on the chair or floor and to your breathing.

Look at the picture and as you do so, direct your breathing towards the image. Imagine your energy flowing out with each out-breath to greet the person who you admire.

As you breathe in, feel the energy which that person offers to you. Feel their strengths and qualities.

As you breathe out, offer your appreciation and gratitude to them.

Enjoy sitting in the presence of the person whom you have chosen. Feel an acknowledgment to them of what they have given to you.

But inspiration is not just about what we gain from having known or read about the other. It is also about appreciating the other as a person who had their own life story and who achieved remarkable things. Such appreciation of other people, for their own sake, takes us out of a self-centred world view and encourages a more mature life stance.

Biography and Family History

Another way of helping people to think more about what their relatives, or other significant people whom they have known, have meant to them is to encourage them to research their lives. With increasing interest in family trees, and ease of access to details through the many sites on the internet, creating a picture of the family can be a rewarding experience, which supports the person in developing the positive aspects of their family story. It can also make them more appreciative of other people's stories, rather than just remaining stuck in their own.

This sort of work becomes particularly valuable where anecdotes and personal details are known, rather than just dates and names. From an initial exploration of the family tree, a person may come across stories of particular people which seem to resonate with their own experience.

Also, researching family history provides an excuse to talk to relatives and particularly the elderly members of the family. This can prove surprisingly rich for young people, who often end up discovering that grandparents or aunts and uncles are far more interesting, and supportive, than they had imagined.

When a person has collected material about a family member, the information and stories can be given further value if they are assembled and presented in an attractive way. Taking care in creating a scrap book or biography, which can maybe later be passed on to other family members, encourages the person making it to value the story they are researching. The process of making a book, or other presentation, adds meaning to the stories which are part of their heritage.

Maureen talks to her aunt and discovers that her great grandmother was born in a small farming community in Derbyshire. With little education, she volunteered for the medical corps during the First World War and served first as an orderly and later, after some training, as a nurse. She worked on the battle field and gained an award for bravery. After the war, she returned to her village, but was unsettled. She became a campaigner for women's rights and was involved in some of the early moves to set up family planning clinics. Despite family opposition, she moved to London where she met and married Maureen's grandfather, a young doctor, four years younger than she was.

When Maureen finds out about her grandmother, she is very impressed by her grandmother's spirit and her willingness to do things which were not approved of by society of her day. Maureen has, herself, fallen out with her mother because she travels a lot and has refused to settle down and get a regular job. She realises that, like her grandmother, she feels drawn to live her life out, following her ideals rather than convention.

Subject matter for such investigations might focus on family history, or might explore the experiences of the family during a particular historical period, for example, prior to leaving their homeland as refugees, or it might produce a biography of one particular person who has been a source of inspiration.

There may be times when you can introduce this kind of activity into your agency setting. Of course, in many cases, it won't be appropriate, but opportunities may arise in surprising ways. A minister who is taking a funeral might encourage the family to create an order of service which incorporates personal reflections on the person who has died. Such a booklet could then act as a small souvenir for those attending. Hospice workers often help a parent who is dying to create memory boxes for children, which might contain stories of grandparents or great grandparents as well as of the parent. A worker supporting a group of refugees might help them to assemble an exhibition of their stories, creating images of the land they have left. A care worker for the elderly might use scrap books as a basis for reminiscence work, or might link up the people in their care to a local history society who were interested in preserving local memories.

EXERCISE NINE: BIOGRAPHICAL WORK
(indeterminate)

Make a scrap book about a member of your family. It might be a person whom you particularly admire or someone who has had an interesting life.

Find an attractive scrap book or drawing book. Collect pictures of the person whom you have chosen and of the places and events that they have experienced in their life. You can also include images which give a flavour of the times in which they lived and other materials which you

---

associate with the person, or indeed anything which will help to bring the pages to life. Be creative. Use colours they would choose, and include anything which will make it personal, like pieces of fabric from favourite clothes, bus tickets or brochures from visits you have made with them, packaging from favourite sweets or biscuits. You can add headlines from newspapers which reflect their interests, or images of people taking part in activities they enjoy or anything else which reminds you of the person.

You might also like to include pieces of writing, either describing incidents from the person's life, or more creative pieces or poems inspired by them. You could include things written by other people about the person – ask other family members.

Try to draw out in the work those qualities which you most admire in your relative. The book can be a tribute. You might like to think about whether the book has a purpose, either as a memento for younger members of the family who perhaps did not know a grandparent, or as a gift for the person themselves. It might take the form of a 'This is Your Life' book to mark a birthday or anniversary.

The people who are important in our lives live with us. Even when we are not in physical contact, their presence affects our thoughts and actions and the way that we see the world. Sometimes the effect that these unseen others have on a person is supportive. Other times, it limits the person and makes them timid or prejudiced. As listeners, our role is to support people in discovering the positive aspects of their relationships, present and past, and to help them to free themselves from the limitations which persist from negative influences.

Session Eight

Relating to Others

This session will include:

- Nei Quan method
- Beyond surviving, reflections on abuse
- Use of sculpting and other representational work
- Seeing through the other person's perspective
- Appreciating difference

As we have seen, the influence which other people have upon our lives is significant. By understanding more about the way that our thinking is conditioned by our patterns of relating, and the ways in which others have been, and can still be, a positive force in shaping our thought, we can grow in confidence and seek out healthier relationships.

All of this can be helpful in supporting people towards creating better conditions in their lives, but it does not necessarily take the person out of their habitual view points. In this session, we will look particularly at ways that you might help someone to get a different perspective and to start to see the other people, with whom they are relating, less in terms of their usefulness or otherwise to ourselves, and more as people who act in their own ways for their own reasons. Of course, this shift is never a complete one, and even when we have an insight of this kind, we inevitably drift back to hanging on to particular views of others, but, in as much as it is possible, it can be very freeing for the person concerned.

This session, then, is primarily focused on methods of working that take a person out of their habitual perspective and encourage them to see other points of view. These methods, drawn from different psychological approaches, all offer practical ways that you can both learn more about the ways in which relationships influence people, and practice skills which will help you to support others in similar investigation.

Nei Quan

Nei Quan (or Naikan as it is also written) is a therapy that originated in Japan, which is based on reflecting on relationships with significant people from our lives. As a method of working, it is interesting in being quite different from most Western therapies. It focuses on primary relationships (i.e. relationships with parents and other similarly significant people). Its effect is generally to help the person who participates in it to reach a point of greater psychological separation from the significant care-giver, who is the subject of the investigation. Let us look at how it is traditionally done.

THE NEI QUAN RETREAT

Traditionally Nei Quan is done in a retreat format. When it is done as an intensive retreat, this takes place over a week or so. Sometimes, however, it is offered in shorter sessions of private contemplation.

Usually the person doing Nei Quan begins by reviewing the earliest period of their life, from birth to three years. This process starts with a focus on the relationship with mother or the person who took on the mothering role. The person is given a set of questions to explore.

The Nei Quan questions are:
- What did this person do for me?
  (e.g. she fed me, washed me, played with me etc)
- What did I do for this person in return?
  (e.g. I hugged her, I folded my clothes)
- What trouble did I, or my presence, cause?

(e.g. she sat with me when I was sick, I wouldn't eat tomatoes)

The person is instructed to work from memory, to be concrete and specific in what they recall and to focus on what actually happened. In particular, they are told not to speculate on psychological factors, but to stay with memories of events and knowledge of what must have been the case. The idea is to recall that meals were cooked or clothes washed but not to speculate on the psychological aspects of the situation or the spirit in which these tasks were done.

Where there is no memory, the person is told to look for evidence from what they know, generally, about caring for a small baby, or about the history of the time in which the events happened. For example, not too long ago women in Britain would normally have had to give up work when a new baby arrived.

The person leading the Nei Quan goes to each participant in turn and invites them to give a report of what they have recalled. The retreat leader will not usually give any comment on what is said, except to encourage the person to continue reflecting. Thus, each participant has a lot of space to explore memories and to think about the truth of their early life. He or she is challenged to keep on looking more closely at the reality of the experience.

After reflecting for a while (maybe half a day) on the first three years of life, the participants in a Nei Quan retreat are moved on to reflect on the next phase of their life (3-6 years). After further time, they go on to the next phase (6-9 years) and so on.

The important thing about Nei Quan is that it is about exploring the reality of the relationship and reaching a deeper appreciation of how it was for the other person. When this happens, we start to see the parent or carer as a separate person with their own life experiences. We see that we were dependent upon them, but that they were not just functional to our lives. They had their own life stories.

The method is not intended to be about blaming anyone, and although people sometimes feel regret and even remorse when undertaking a Nei Quan retreat, most people predominantly feel appreciation and gratitude and a sense of release.

EXERCISE ONE: NEI QUAN MEDITATION
(twenty minutes)

Spend twenty minutes doing Nei Quan. Sit in your quiet space. You may have a pad of paper and writing materials beside you and you may record any memories which come to you. Write down concrete incidents that you remember or things which you know must have happened. (Do not get side-tracked into writing about personal process, thoughts or feelings.) Not everything that you write needs to be written from memory, but you need to be fairly sure that it is true.

Choose one parent, probably your mother if she was your main carer. Reflect on your relationship with that parent over the first five years of your life.
• What did your parent do for you?
• What did you do in return?
• What trouble did you cause?

After twenty minutes, read through your notes and spend ten minutes in meditation, holding that parent in your thoughts.

Record your reflections.

HOW MIGHT NEI QUAN BE RELEVANT TO THE LISTENER?
Nei Quan is probably not a practice which you will teach to

people with whom you work, but it will give you insight into a different way of thinking about relationships. It is something which you might like to use yourself.

First of all, it may be helpful to you in understanding your own relationships better. Secondly, in a more general way, it may help you to develop more of a sense of the factors which impinge on other people's lives. Thirdly, it can give you a feel for the sorts of questions that can help a person to move out of a self-orientated perspective (which can trap them into negative cycles of thinking) into seeing other people in a fresh way. You might ask someone, "So what was your mother doing at that time?" or, "It must have been tough for your mother on her own with four small children, did you all help out?"

You might introduce this way of thinking into a conversation with somebody whom you are supporting (person A). For example, you might sometimes enquire about the situation of a third party (person B) who is being talked about, asking what they (B) are doing and how they (B) experience your client (A)'s problems. In doing this, you may help the person with whom you are talking (A) to move beyond their pre-conceptions and investigate the reality of the lives of other people, thus getting out of a narrow world view.

Some of the other methods which we will use in this session will also show you ways in which you can encourage people to look at the experiences of significant people in their lives and to see them from a different perspective. These may offer a similar experience to Nei Quan.

ADAPTING NEI QUAN TO EVERYDAY LISTENING SITUATIONS

Traditionally Nei Quan is a method which involves reflection on the care-givers who supported us in childhood, but you can also work with the Nei Quan questions to reflect on people to whom you relate in your current life.

One way of doing this is to reflect back over the past twenty-four hours and think of all that you have received during this time. This might include reflecting on people who you work with, on family and friends, on the strangers who serve us in shops or health services or transport, and on the people we never meet who provide infrastructure to our society. It might also include reflecting on the things which you receive from the natural world, like air and sunlight, growth processes and warmth. You can ask, "What did they do for me? What did I do in return? What trouble did my existence cause for them?"

Nei Quan makes us more aware of the importance of our relationships. In particular, it makes us aware of how much we depend on others in practical ways and that the balance of our lives is such that we receive far more than we give out.

EXERCISE TWO: COLLAGE ON NEI QUAN THEMES
(half an hour)

Create a collage representing the past twenty-four hours. Use any pictures, coloured paper, and scraps of cloth or bric-a-brac. Show what you have received during that time.

Create a second collage of what you have given out, both the positive things which you gave to others and the difficulties which your presence caused.

Place the two collages in front of you and reflect upon them.

Beyond Surviving: Reflecting on Abuse

People sometimes ask what effect Nei Quan has on people who have experienced serious abuse. Surely the person who has been badly treated or neglected by a parent does not wish to spend time reflecting on what that person did for them?

As a listener you may well come across people who have experienced serious abuse, whether physical, sexual or emotional, in childhood or more recently. How should you support a person in this situation?

Understandably, people who have this sort of childhood history are not initially going to be ready to explore the experience of the people who were perpetrators in an abusive relationship. The biggest need of such a person at this stage is simply to be listened to. Frequently people in this position have not talked much about their history. The abuse is often something which a person has felt ashamed of. Experiences of abuse may be buried in layers of blame and guilt. The person may feel that what happened was their own fault, or else that the person who abused them was a monster. They may be troubled by images and half remembered incidents which return to haunt them in dreams or flashbacks (vivid waking dream-like states in which the person re-lives the incidents).

The process of moving beyond such experiences goes through many phases. It may involve swinging between self-blame and blaming the other person. As listener, your most important function is in providing a steady and non-directive presence. This will create the space for the person to explore and start to integrate their experience. Different emotions will flow as memories become unfrozen and things which may have been held secretly for years are brought into the light.

Often a person caught in such emotions needs more support than a listener can give, in which case, encourage the person to seek help from a counsellor or therapist. If the person has never confided in anyone before, their emotions may reach a point of such turmoil that they seem to lose touch with reality, and you may feel it is best for someone who is more experienced to take over. At the same time, such support is not always available, and even if it is, the person may also be involved with you in some other context. They may trust you and not be willing to talk to anyone else. They may want to talk to you.

EXERCISE THREE: SUPPORTING SOMEONE WHO HAS EXPERIENCED ABUSE
(ten minutes)

Imagine yourself in the situation where somebody confides in you about traumatic experiences which happened to them in childhood. Perhaps they were abused sexually. Perhaps they have never told anyone before. Perhaps they experienced torture or mutilation.

How would you respond? How easy would you find it to stay grounded as they talked? At what point might you feel you needed to refer the person on to a counsellor or other professional? How would you do this?

It may be that you have already been in this sort of situation. If so, reflect on how you handled it and whether you might behave differently on another occasion.

Make notes on your responses, then, if this is something which you are new to, take some time to read some accounts written by people who experienced sexual and other abuse. You will find plenty of books on the subject available, which include autobiographical accounts of childhood abuse. As you read, try to get a sense of what the writer might be experiencing as they write, what they are trying to achieve by sharing the experience, and whether their perceptions of the experience have shifted over time.

One of the most valuable things which you can offer is your ability to ground yourself. If you can be a stable point for the person, they will find their own way through the feelings in most cases. The person needs a supportive presence so that they can heal through their own process.

This process is basically one in which the person seeks to understand and make sense of their experiences. Early on, the memories may feel overwhelming and they feel the need of some distance. The impact of the abuser is still powerful, and the person is still psychologically enmeshed with them. Later there will come a point when the person it ready to get some distance from the abuser.

Exploring the reality of that person's life, they may start to make sense of what happened. They may start to appreciate that the abuser had his or her reasons for acting as they did. Those reasons might not be good ones, but they had nothing really to do with the person who was abused. They were embedded in the abuser's conditions.

Realising this can be very liberating. The person no longer feels as caught up with their tormentor. They will probably never like the person or approve of their behaviour, but they may well see a pathetic old man or a sad, angry woman, or a lonely tyrant. They can then make sense of their experiences and move on.

Sculpting

Nei Quan offers a way of looking at relationships through the use of particular questions which focus on finding out about the reality of a situation. Another way of exploring relationships is through a method called *sculpting*. This uses objects such as counters or stones to represent relationships between people or things. The objects are placed on a flat surface in relationship with one another. Through sculpting we can explore, for example, the relationships between different people in a family or other social group. The objects used might all be of the same kind, but might be different things. For example you might use a set of small toys. They are usually small so that a sculpt can be done on a table top, but it is an infinitely adaptable method.

Although it sounds somewhat artificial, in fact, people often naturally use sculpting techniques in conversations when they want to explain something complicated. A person sitting in a café might use coffee cups, spoons, salt pots and other items to show relationships between people at a recent family event. Someone in a pub might use beer mats and glasses to explain the progress of a football game. A teenage girl might use coins from her purse to explain the changing relationships between different people in her social circle.

This sort of visual representation helps to make what is being said clearer. When we can see the connections between people mapped out and can try moving the objects around to experiment with different permutations, things about the relationships may become apparent.

Because this kind of visual representation of relationships is something which people often do naturally, it can easily be introduced into a listening conversation. There is no need for you, as the listener, to spend time explaining what you are going to do. You can simply collect a few things from around the room and say "show me." For example, if the person is getting muddled in trying to explain family relationships to you, you could take out some loose change and work out the family structure between you.

If you like using sculpting, sometimes it is nice to have suitable objects to hand. A basket of pebbles on a window sill can be there as a decoration until they are needed for this kind of work. You might use coins from your pocket, or carry a small bag of buttons or a little bag of 'worry dolls'.

Sculpting is helpful because:

- It helps you to keep track of complicated relationships. If you are talking with someone who is telling you about a lot of different relatives or friends, sculpting can help you to be clear about relationships. Often, through sculpting, things become apparent which have been glossed over. For example, it may be obvious that the person has missed one family member out of their description of an event, or that there is some family dynamic being enacted which they have not mentioned.
- It shows you things about particular relationships that might not be said. You might notice that two objects representing a couple are actually placed a long way apart, for example.
- Both the objects themselves and the position they are put in give information. For example, the things chosen to represent people may be very different in size or quality. You might notice that some objects are placed a long way away from the one representing the person who is making the sculpt, or a long way from each other. All of these details tell you something about the person's life and relationships.
- Patterns become apparent. You might notice groups of objects, or repeating patterns where different groups mirror one another.
- It is fun to do.

Of course, sculpting has some things in common with some of the drawing exercises which we have already used, but it has the advantage that it uses objects which can be moved around or which can be picked up and held. This means that you can often learn more from a sculpt than you can from a drawing. It also avoids the self-consciousness which many people feel in relation to drawing.

EXERCISE FOUR: SCULPTING

(five minutes)

The objects chosen to create a sculpt can be significant.

Imagine that the objects in the picture above represent a family. Which do you think might be the mother, the father and the child? What associations might they have for you?

If you were choosing to sculpt your own family using these objects, which ones would you choose to represent which family member? Looking round your room, which objects can you see which you would add to complete your sculpt? Reflect on the personal meaning of the objects for you.

FACILITATING SOMEONE IN MAKING A SCULPT

If you are encouraging someone to use objects to show you relationships in this way, keep the things which you say to a minimum. Don't try to interpret the meaning of things, but simply observe and comment on what you actually see. The temptation with this sort of work is to try to offer clever insights about what is being represented, but it is much better to let the person find their own understanding.

You might say things like:

- I notice that you have put those three stones very close together.
- I am wondering why you chose a blue counter to represent Mary.
- I see you have not put your aunt's husband in. Did she not marry after all?
- You have used the same coins to represent yourself and your grandmother, do you feel a special connection with her?
- If you were to change this so that it shows things as you would like them to be,
- what would you do?

You will notice that none of these responses tells the person who is making the sculpt what the objects might represent. They simply ask questions or invite the person to explore further.

Sculpts do not have to be used to represent people. Sometimes they can be useful for investigating other elements in a person's life. You might use a sculpt to look at which subjects a person enjoys most at school, with a view to looking at which they might want to specialise in. You might use a sculpt to look at the different feelings which a person had about a situation, using objects to represent the thoughts and emotions which they associated with it. You might use a sculpt to plan a timetable of events or a bit exhibition.

EXERCISE FIVE: FAMILY SCULPTS
(twenty minutes)

Experiment with making sculpts of your present family or social network. Try using different objects and see what difference it makes using objects of different sizes or types.

When you have made your sculpt, record it either by drawing it or by taking a photograph.

Now try moving elements in your sculpt so that you can look at different ways of developing the scenario.
- How will it look in five years time?
- How would it look if a key person moved away?
- How would it look if you had an argument with one of the other people?
- How would you ideally like it to look?

If you have the opportunity, experiment with working with a partner, taking turns to facilitate each other in turn in creating sculpts. Practice using a reflective style of response and questions which focus the other person's attention on details without imposing your interpretation of what the sculpt might represent.

Seeing Through the Other Person's Eyes

When someone is finding a relationship difficult and views have become entrenched, it can sometimes be helpful to encourage them to try to look at the world through the other person's eyes.

One way of doing this might be to build on the sculpting method. You could point to the object in the sculpt which represents the other person, or even pick it up, and ask "What do you think this looks like from her point of view?" You could even develop this by saying "If she were making a sculpt of the situation, what would it look like?" and inviting the person to show you.

This switch of viewpoint, from the person's own perspective to that of the other party, is called *role-reversal*. It can be very helpful in allowing people to move out of their habitual patterns of thinking. If you can get the person to put themselves into the other person's shoes and really see things and think about the situation the way the other person does, it may bring about real changes in the relationship.

Whilst there are techniques for doing this sort of work, in the ordinary listening situation, things will probably unfold more naturalistically. You can encourage people to make the shift into the other's point of view and look at other perspectives in ordinary conversation, using open-ended questions and reflections.

When someone tells you about a third party you might say things like:

- I'm wondering how he sees this.
- What might John say?
- It sounds as if Mary is feeling angry about this.
- I'm thinking there may be something she wants from you…

All of these encourage the person with whom you are talking to start to think about the other person's perspective. They encourage role-reversal. You can extend the investigation of the other person's perspective by asking more about the other person:

- Does she like her work?
- What clothes is she most comfortable in?
- What sort of family has she got?
- Where did she live as a child?
- What are her views on politics, art, or music?

It is often the incidental details of a person's life which bring them alive. Being curious about the other person, you may encourage the person you are talking with to see the situation they are describing through the other person's eyes and so become more appreciative of their viewpoint.

EXERCISE SIX: EXPLORING ROLE REVERSAL
(twenty minutes)

Choose one of the people whom you have been investigating in one of the previous exercises in this session. Take a sheet of paper and sit at a table to write.

Imagine that you (A) are the person (B) who you have decided to investigate. Think about how they (B) would sit at the table, and try to adopt their body posture. Think about how (B) would approach a writing task. Would (B) enjoy it, or resist it? What sort of language would you, as (B), express yourself in?

Now (as person B) write about your life;
- What is important to you?
- What events stand out?
- What relationships are good?
- How do you see person (A)?

When you have finished writing, put the paper down and check to see whether there are any residual thoughts or feelings which belong to the role (B), then get up and walk around the room. Come out of role and be yourself (A). Take the paper to a different place in the room and read it.

Reflect on the exercise. How easy was it to imagine your way into the role of the other person? Were there things which helped you to do this? What did you learn about how things look to that person? Did the exercise tell you things which you had not learned from previous investigations?

Appreciating Difference

People often find it difficult to acknowledge differences. It is quite common for community groups to assert their commonality and, if they do talk about people who are different, to do so in a way which excludes them. Even where differences are obvious, such as when people are of different ages, racial backgrounds, or faiths, there is a strong tendency for people to underplay the distinctions and comment that "We're all the same really."

This is a pity, since difference can be a rich resource and a group which includes people from diverse backgrounds is much more interesting and fulfilling to be a part of. Each person has their own story and, together, they create a patchwork of complimentary colours.

There are a number of specific problems in asserting commonality:

- The assertion of similarity tends to gloss over features which make the group members special.
- It can also leave members feeling unheard.
- The culture of the most numerous or most powerful members tends to predominate.
- The group minimises rather than maximises its capacity.
- A message is conveyed that difference is something to be feared.
- People do not really get to know one another.

The avoidance of difference often comes from a mistaken belief that treating everyone with equal respect means treating them all the same. As a group facilitator you might encourage people to be more positive about their differences by saying things like:

- It sounds as if we have a number of perspectives on this.

- So Mary would like to go to London whilst Barbara and Joan would prefer the country.
- I really appreciate the rich variety of opinions this group is expressing.
- Can we collect as many different possibilities as possible?
- Perhaps we can arrange a series of cookery/craft/sports evenings so different people can teach us their skills.
- I can see we are not going to agree on this, so perhaps we can just agree to differ.
- It sounds as if you are really upset that John doesn't agree with you.

EXERCISE SEVEN: REFLECTING ON DIFFERENCE IN GROUPS
(ten minutes)

Think about groups which you have been involved with. How have they coped with differences between members? What effect has this had?

If you are working in a group, how are you dealing with differences within your current group? What differences do you think exist? Are they acknowledged?

You might like to use a stone passing at this point to explore your sense of difference within the group. If you do, encourage each group member to be aware of what they feel able to say, and what they censor.

Make notes of your experience.

Session Nine

Not Judging

This session will include:

- Ordinariness and dependence on others
- The myth of perfection
- The roots of criticalness
- Unconditional Positive Regard
- Fellow feeling
- Feeling guilty

In the last session we looked at the way that each person has their own story. People are all different. Their idiosyncrasies make them interesting. Their faults make them human. We are rarely attracted to people who seem to be too good. Perhaps we don't trust them because we think there must be a catch. No one is *really* that good. Perhaps they show us up by comparison. Perhaps they are just not very interesting. People's rough edges are part of their charm. We are more attracted to the lovable rogue than the paragon of virtue.

Yet at the same time, many people are not satisfied with themselves. In this paradoxical age, we do not believe in heroes and yet we cling to a myth of progress and the possibility of achieving perfection. People feel eaten up with ambition or crippled with guilt. They struggle to change, experimenting with every new diet, physical or mental. They are reluctant to accept that they are ordinary.

The mode of thinking, which emphasises our ordinariness instead of our specialness, goes against the grain of much modern thinking. On the other hand, it is by no means a pessimistic view. Besides being realistic, it offers a perspective which removes two of the great psychological difficulties of modern life. It refutes the idea that we should strive for perfection and it supports a radically non-judgemental view. This session will explore these aspects of ordinariness and will look at how the listener can support people in resisting the pressures which they feel to attain impossible goals.

Being Ordinary, Being Dependent

We rely on other people to provide us with the ordinary things in life. It is so easy to take these things for granted, but without a lot of ordinary help, we would find it very difficult to maintain even a normal level of functioning.

Just imagine how it would be if you had to grow all your own food, prepare it from scratch, even prepare the utensils to do this with. Imagine cutting all the wood you would need to heat your home – or, for that matter, building your home using raw materials taken from the hills and woodlands like our ancestors did. Imagine making all your clothes from raw cotton or wool, and looking after the sheep or the cotton plants.

Once we start to think in this way, we become much more aware of the way that our modern society depends on each person doing their part and contributing to the whole. Each of us is very dependent on others. Realising this, we are likely to feel much more appreciation and gratitude to others.

This dependence is not just at an individual level though. It is sobering to think about the way that Western countries have become far more dependant than some of the poorer countries, where people live closer to the land and produce their own food. How much do we, as a nation, do to provide for ourselves? If you look at where most goods are produced, it is easy to see that, if we were cut off from other nations, we would soon be in difficulties.

> *Thought: What impact do you think it has on people's mind states living in a country that takes so much from other countries and which would have great difficulty providing for its own needs through its own manufacturing?*

At the same time, the poorer countries are also tied into a system in which they depend on Western finance and know-how and are gradually reducing their capacities to be self-sufficient, albeit at a subsistence level, as they enter world markets.

Ultimately, though, we all depend on the environment, on the natural processes of the planet and the universe and on whatever lies beyond it. We are at the mercy of natural disasters and recipients of natural gifts.

The fact that we depend on others in this way does not mean, however, that other people are all saints. They are ordinary people like us, also dependent on others for their support.

When we really see this, we may feel moved by the vulnerability of people whom we thought to be powerful and self-sufficient. We may recognise that they, like us, are struggling to do their best in circumstances which are often less than ideal.

EXERCISE ONE: INVESTIGATING DEPENDENCY
(twenty minutes)

Listen to a news broadcast on the radio. Ideally, record it or use 'listen again' so that you can listen several times.

What sorts of items are included? What do they say about our dependency on one another, on other countries, on the environment and so on?

Reflect on how stories are presented. What point of view is implicit in the reporting? How apparent or otherwise is our dependency? Who is portrayed as being in the right or in the better situation? What sort of language is used, and does the choice of words carry implications about the view of the reporter or news programme?

What messages do you think the news broadcast conveys implicitly to listeners? Does it promote anxiety or calm? Does it give balance to all the parties mentioned? Does it support a sense of entitlement or superiority?

Think of somebody whom you have worked with, or know socially, who comes from another country with a different culture, maybe one that is in the news. Listen to the broadcast a second time and reflect on how different it might sound to that person. If you have opportunities to hear broadcasts from different countries' news or broadcasts aimed at different cultural groups, compare the style of reporting and the different implicit messages they contain.

The Myth of Perfection

One of the problems of modern life is that we are surrounded by images in magazines, on television, and on advertising hoardings, of people who look perfect and live in beautiful homes, with neat, tidy families, who grow up achieving accolades along the way. It is easy to feel that we should be living up to these standards.

Most book shops stock many self-help books, advertising that they will help the reader to achieve improvement in almost any conceivable area of life. If something is wrong, there is a means to correct it, we are told.

EXERCISE TWO: LOSING CONFIDENCE
(ten minutes)

Mira works in a responsible management job. She lives in a pleasant flat which she shares with her boyfriend. Next year they plan to marry. Mira has a first class degree and is studying for a master's degree in her spare time. She has always done well academically. Now Mira comes to talk with you. She is suffering from anxiety attacks which are preventing her from sleeping and she feels that, although other people think she is doing well, she is not doing anything with her life. She feels useless and is terrified that she will show everyone what a fraud she really is.

How would you respond to Mira?

We cannot know what was really going on for Mira, but, using your imagination, write a short description of what you think might lie behind her feeling of being a fraud?

Have you known anyone like Mira? What do you think affected their confidence?

At work, people struggle to meet increasingly heavy deadlines, and to hold their own in competitive environments where status and achievement are valued. People are forced to seek more and more qualifications in order to maintain the same position. Not only this, but often people are trying to juggle their work with an active home life in which leisure time is also increasingly structured.

If there is an accident, someone must be responsible. We must see that it never happens again. Everything must be insured against. As each new potential risk emerges, the pressure to cover every possible eventuality increases costs and anxieties. Regulations increase and innovation is restricted.

It is part of the modern myth that, in the face of all this, we should be self-reliant and confident.

Against these pressures, it is not surprising that some people feel overwhelmed or simply slip between the rails of social provision. Alongside the emphasis on self-reliance, a drive towards independence and autonomy has created a society in which increasing numbers of people live alone. The vast numbers of single person households and those run by lone parents include some individuals who choose and relish the freedom which such a lifestyle can offer, at least to the better off, but they also include others who are unhappy casualties of a trend which has diminished the value placed on community.

Implications for Listeners

As a listener, you may meet some people like Mira, whom society views as successful, but you are also likely to meet many for whom ideals of independence and personal autonomy would ring very hollow, if they even thought about life in such terms. For such people, existence is lonely and unfulfilling, scratched out in the narrow confines of second class or non-existent services and poor living conditions.

You will meet others who feel brow beaten by the pressure they feel from social expectations, feeling that they should live up to some ideal which is always out of reach. They may feel burdened by failure or guilt and be convinced that other people are living the sort of life to which they aspire.

EXERCISE THREE: REFLECTIONS ON SOCIAL TRENDS

(ten minutes)

Do you agree that social problems are created by the pressure towards independence, achievement and autonomy? Does it impact on you personally?

What sort of social trends affect the people with whom you work? Make some notes on your thoughts on this topic.

In hearing different people's stories, we can feel swept into their different worlds, torn between different perspectives and emotions. With one person, we may feel caught by the enthusiasm of their ambition, with another, we may feel sunk in the despair and feelings of futility of trying to achieve standards which are impossibly high. With a third, we may feel drawn into anger and bitterness at a system which seems to be failing the ordinary people.

On the one hand, these energies are the fuel of people's lives. They may give the person impetus to make positive changes. On the other hand, if they are grounded in a false view of what is possible, we may feel torn in our support, wanting to affirm whatever positive energy the person has, but at the same time, seeing the destructive influence which such aspirations can have.

The role of listener may be to hold a space where something less than perfect is acceptable. The person themselves may sense that the internal voices which urge constant effort are unreasonable, but may need support to defy them. Hearing those quieter voices which encourage the person to accept what is, and drawing them out, may be important.

In other cases, listeners may have a role in supporting people to campaign for real changes in their circumstances. In local community settings, the campaigning group can be an important catalyst both for bringing about the improvements they seek and for creating community cohesion and validation. Of course getting involved in campaigning has its costs to the role of listener, and if a worker becomes too deeply involved in fighting on local issues, their neutrality and availability to some members of the community may be compromised.

EXERCISE FOUR: REFLECTIONS ON ROLE AND SUPPORTING CAMPAIGNS
(five minutes)

Reflect on your role in the particular setting where you are involved. Are there ways in which you can support those who, for one reason or another, feel cut out of main-stream society?

If so, how do you do it?

Do you see it as part of your role as listener to work in bringing about social change? Do you get involved in other sorts of social action? If you were to get involved in local or national campaigns for better conditions for the people with whom you are working, would this benefit them or would it, in some ways, create conflicts within that role?

If you do not get involved in campaigns, what effect might this have?

Being Bombu and Critical Nature

A useful concept for thinking about people's ordinariness is the term *bombu*. This Japanese term refers to the ordinary person. More literally, it is part of a longer phrase which translates as a *foolish being of wayward passion*. We are all bombu. No matter how hard anyone tries, they will always make mistakes and sometimes mess things up and have nasty moods. We all have passions which are mostly kept under wraps or channelled in socially acceptable ways, but sometimes, unpredictably, they break out. This is because we all have histories. We have a whole lot of previous experiences, bad habits and conditioned ways of seeing things. These mean that we don't always see situations clearly. Our personal baggage makes it very difficult for us to be to be consistently wise and loving to everyone.

The importance of this idea, in the context of listening to others, is that, if we take it seriously, we are likely to find a much more kindly way of seeing others' faults, as well as our own. The concept of bombu nature pushes us towards an attitude which is much less judgemental. When people are caught up in thinking that they should always get it right, they become critical of themselves. This leads them to be critical of others as well. Trying to be perfect often conditions a judgemental mentality.

EXERCISE FIVE: LOOKING AT CRITICALNESS (1)
(five minutes)

Think about ways in which you are critical of yourself. You might think of things like:
- Not liking your appearance
- Being dissatisfied with your educational achievements
- Feeling that you have said something silly when you

---

speak in a meeting
- Not wanting to drive in front of other people
- Thinking that you can't ask for promotion because you aren't good enough
- Being cross with yourself for not having asked for promotion
- Being embarrassed to show the report you have written
- Wishing that you didn't blush when you are embarrassed
- Blaming yourself for choosing partners who let you down
- Hating yourself for having an extra helping of ice cream
- Feeling that you have made a mess of a listening skills exercise

And so on....

What do you least like about yourself?

What effect do you think your view of your own behaviour has on your ability to listen to others?

Being self-critical may:
- Make us critical of others whom we see as having the same fault as we have, or as being even being worse than we are.
- Make us defensive and determined not to let others see our faults (and so not get to know us.)
- Make us self-preoccupied, unconfident and unwilling to have a go at doing things for fear of failing.

The fact that we recognise the problems which arise from being too self-critical does not mean we need to go to the other extreme and tell ourselves that we are perfect. It does not mean that we should stop trying to avoid hurting others or behaving badly. Rather, it means that we do so from a position of knowing that our failings are part of our being human, and appreciating that, even as we try to improve matters in one area of our lives, we are bound to carry on slipping up in other ways.

Sometimes, we are not even aware that our criticalness of others comes out of our own self-criticism. We have become so used to the background voices of criticism, that we just assume that this is normal. We go about the world viewing everything with a critical eye, noticing all the ways that people fail to come up to the standards which we have taken on and becoming irritated with them. The thing which we find most irritating in others is often the thing that we are struggling with in ourselves.

Not only do we blame other people for not coming up to standard, sometimes we may also resent the fact that they seem less concerned about what they are doing than we are. It may be that in seeing how different they are from us, we imagine that they are free from the voices which haunt us, and we envy them.

EXERCISE SIX: LOOKING AT CRITICALNESS (2)
(five minutes)

Take a large sheet of paper and divide it into two columns. At the top of the first column write 'other people' and at the top of the second column write 'myself'.

Now think about a person who you find irritating. Think about what it is that you find difficult about them. Try to recall actual incidents when your irritation arose. Make a list of them. (Don't be afraid to say what it is you find difficult about them.)

Now, in the second column, take each incident and write down ways in which you might act similarly or ways in which you would act differently.

Identify ways in which your own self-criticism may be affecting your view of the other person, maybe causing resentment about how they are.

Unconditional Positive Regard

Just as you are
Really
Just as you are

Inagaki

This little poem by the Japanese poet, Inagaki, summarises the response that is completely free from judgement. It is the response to the bombu person. Of course, as ordinary people, we never *can* be completely non-judgemental. Being free from judgementalism is an ideal and something which belongs to the realm of the spiritual and the eternal rather than the human, but we can be aware of our tendency to judge and try to minimise it.

Carl Rogers, an American psychologist, who developed a lot of the theory and ideas which underlie modern counselling, spoke of the importance of, what he called, *unconditional positive regard*. One way of thinking about unconditional positive regard is to think in terms of creating space for people. If we can create a space in ourselves so that we listen to the other person without imposing our views or trying to direct them, and if we do this with a warm, open presence, we make it possible for the person to talk. This is unconditional positive regard.

According to Rogers' model, unconditional positive regard is one of a set of conditions which make personal change possible. Often these are presented as three *core conditions*. The other two core conditions are *empathy* and *congruence*. Empathy means the listener's ability to stand in the other's shoes and see things from their perspective. Congruence means being genuine and not just responding because you have learned a technique or are playing a role.

Working with these conditions can provide a lifetime of learning as, when we go deeper into them, we discover that there are more and more layers of pretence. We become more and more aware of the misunderstanding and distortion in our view of the other. As we develop in each of these areas, we are likely to naturally become more humble in our self-assessment and, in consequence, become more compassionate in our judgement of others. Unconditional positive regard of others starts to be born out of a more realistic self-assessment.

EXERCISE SEVEN: EXPLORING OUR TENDENCY TO JUDGE
(fifteen minutes)

Listen to a couple of different speakers recorded from a radio or television programme.

As you listen, keep a check list in front of you and mark down the points where you feel judgemental reactions arising in you and points where you notice yourself feeling more sympathetic.

You can do this as a sort of graph, mapping rises and falls

---

in your regard for the person as they speak.

When you have finished, reflect back over the points where you lost sympathy and identify what caused this to happen. Did you have a personal investment in them being different, either because of your own struggles or because of ideals which you hold?

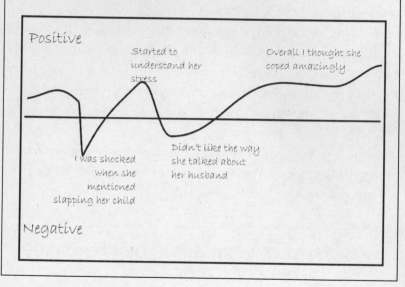

Offering unconditional listening gives the other person the opportunity to share their story and all their thoughts and feelings without expecting that they will be judged. People are often very sensitive to others' judgements. Because many of us have been criticised a lot, we learn to notice the early signs of disapproval and we shape what we say accordingly. We will not really be open with the other person. To really trust another person we must feel they will not judge us too harshly.

Whilst we can't always avoid being judgemental, we can reduce our tendencies to judge by:

- Being aware that we do tend to judge others.
- Wanting to be less judgemental.
- Developing empathy for the other person.
- Recognising that we are ourselves *bombu* and that we slip up all the time.

Fellow Feeling

When we recognise that others also feel vulnerable and when we accept that we have ordinary human quirks and failings and stop being determined to eliminate them at all costs, we become more sympathetic to the situations which other people get themselves into. We are far less likely to feel condemnatory or think "how could they do that!" or "why don't they just sort themselves out?" We know from our own experience that life just isn't that simple. When we stop approaching others from a position of implicit superiority, we are much more able to appreciate their struggles, even if they are different from our own. We develop the kind of attitude to those whom we help which we call fellow feeling.

Fellow feeling means we have a stance of 'that could be me' or 'there by the grace of God go I'. It does not necessarily mean we think the other person was right or that we condone what they have done, but it does mean that we appreciate that even the most awful behaviours come out of human frailty, which all of us have. We no longer feel judgmental towards the man who comes in and talks about the fight he had last night. We just feel sorry for his injured hand, concern for the other person involved and empathy for his anxiety about whether the police will press charges. We hope he will learn from the experience, not because we feel condemnatory towards him, but because we care for the pain he is going through. We understand the pain which comes from having let our passions get out of control.

From the position of fellow feeling we can work together to find ways for the person to understand the ramifications of what has happened, to make amends if necessary, or change their behaviour in the future. We no longer need to condemn or to pretend that the incident did not happen.

Feeling Guilty

People feel guilty for a variety of reasons. Sometimes someone may want to talk with you about how they feel guilty. A carer may feel guilty because they feel they are not doing enough. They may feel guilty for not always being willing and sweet tempered. A mother may feel guilty for scolding her child, or smacking him. A teenage girl may feel guilty for having sex with her boyfriend. A man may feel guilty for killing someone in a drink drive accident. A parent may feel guilty because their child died in the car accident.

As you can see from these examples, sometimes, when a person feels guilty, they really are guilty. They may have done something which, on reflection, they now consider wrong, or they may have knowingly acted badly. Such guilt is objective.

Other times when people feel guilty, there is nothing which they have done that anyone would think of as wrong. The source of guilt may be trivial, or the feeling of guilt may not seem to be founded on any actual deed at all, but rather to be a more nebulous sense of unworthiness or culpability, or it may be out of proportion with what has been done.

Sometimes the situation is complicated, and the person has, with good intention, got caught up in actions which have proved harmful to someone.

PROVIDING A LISTENING SPACE

When someone feels overwhelmed with guilt, one of their greatest needs is simply to be listened to. If you can listen without judging, you will be able to provide a clean space in which the person can talk about what they have done and find their own conclusions without you:

- judging them and losing empathy
- telling them they did the right thing when they didn't

Our ability to provide such a non-judgemental space comes out of our fellow feeling. We know that we could also have made similar or equivalent mistakes. Also, we have a deep empathy for the conditions of the person's life which led to the event. When we really get a feel for the sort of pressures which another person is under, we are far less likely to leap to quick conclusions about their behaviour.

RECOUNTING WHAT HAPPENED

When we have done something that we regret and feel guilty about, there are often two conflicting impulses. One is to hide what we have done and pretend it did not happen. The other is to confess and 'get it off our chest'. As a person feels more trust in the listener, their guard will start to drop and they may start to feel less need to defend themselves. Telling the story of the event can be very releasing.

As listener, you may feel a deep appreciation of the trust which the other person is putting in you by telling you about their feelings of guilt. You may feel that they are making a confession. The appreciation which arises outweighs any critical feelings which one might have about the incident.

FEELING JUDGEMENTAL

Of course, occasionally, someone may tell you something which leaves you feeling uneasy. You may need to struggle to contain your feelings. Here too it may be helpful to look into the reaction and ask what lies behind it. Perhaps it arises from some personal memory or attitude which has been evoked.

Maybe as a woman, you feel uncomfortable when the person

speaking expresses misogynistic views. Maybe as a pacifist, you feel disturbed by confessions of violence, real or fantasised. If the roots of our feelings of judgement are personal, linked to our own experiences of past hurt, there is probably an immediate need to re-establish our empathy for the person who is talking. Listening more carefully to their experience may help to take us out of our concerns.

At the same time, these things are complicated, because the person who is talking may be saying something which he or she knows will shock you. The person may, at some level, want to find out how you will react, seeing if you can be trusted, or provoked into an angry response. On the other hand, the person may just assume that you share their world view, or that you have particular views which fit a stereotype of the kind of person they believe you are. These dynamics may mean that what is said has more to do with your relationship with the person you are helping than with the subject being talked about.

Sometimes, though, we may feel that we need to challenge what is being said. All of us will have limits to what we are willing to listen to. Exactly where each person draws the line will vary. For example, if a person is racist or offensive in their speech, we may need to set a limit and ask them to stop.

EXERCISE EIGHT: JUDGEMENTS

(five minutes)

How would you respond to the following comments from service users?
- You women are all the same.
- These Poles are taking all of our jobs.
- I've ****ing had enough.
- Don't you tell me what to do!
- I hate gays.

- Women should expect to be raped wearing those short skirts.

Think about comments which you would not be prepared to tolerate and what you would say to a person who made them.

Rarely, someone may tell us something which raises real concerns. If there is threat of violence or an issue relating to abuse of children, we may be bound to take action. We may have responsibilities to a third party, as in the case where a child is at risk. We may need to report an incident to authorities or take other action. This does not, however, need to stop us from feeling understanding for the mother's situation and reasons for acting as she does. If we can have such understanding, we are more likely to help her and prevent further abuse happening.

So, in such a situation, preserving the sense of fellow feeling is still important. We can empathise with someone's struggles without agreeing and we can support someone from an appreciation of the human dilemmas of their situation and still take the matter to the appropriate authority. It is not easy, but keeping our concern for the person to the fore, and being honest about our duties and the reasons for them, is the only way that we can hold them through what will be a painful process.

Often, though, our feelings of judgement are simply reflections of the other person's own self-critical thoughts. We catch their perception of their faults and buy into their self-condemnation. A search for the truth in our hearts and in the reality of the other person's situation may reveal such layers of negativity.

HONEST EXPLORATION AND REPARATION

Having told the story of the event or events, it then becomes possible for the person to explore the reality of their situation. How do they assess their actions now, looking back at what happened? Did they do the right thing? What else might they have done? Did they get it wrong? Were they guilty?

Facing reality is the first step to letting go of the feelings of guilt. Having looked at the reality, a person may then have a sense of whether they need to do anything to make reparation for their actions. This might involve an apology to someone who has been hurt, or making recompense to them in some way.

Supporting a person to face the consequences of their actions, and to find a way to resolve the aftermath of them, breaks the cycle of self-condemnation, guilt and self-justification which can continue indefinitely.

NOT FALSELY REASSURING

Simply reassuring a person that they are not to blame when this is not true is not often helpful. It stops the person talking about their unease and prevents them making an honest exploration of the reality of the situation.

- Sometimes, feeling guilty is the result of a person having standards which are too high. The person is trying to be perfect. Helping the person to talk may lead to them reassessing these expectations and becoming more realistic about their capacities.
- Sometimes, feeling guilty is about feeling we have let ourselves down. It is a way of punishing ourselves. A lot of pride can be caught up in guilt. Offering acceptance of the person, and appreciating that we are all fallible, may help the person to forgive him or herself for what happened and look on the whole matter more lightly.
- Sometimes, feeling guilty is realistic. When this is so, we need to think about what needs to happen to improve matters. If some reparation is possible and desirable, encouraging the

person to get on and do it will be more helpful than carrying on talking about their feelings of guilt. It is also a good test of whether the person really feels regret of if they are just 'making the right noises'.

- Sometimes, feeling guilty may mean we have broken someone else's taboo or rules and are afraid of their judgement. In this case, the person who feels guilty probably needs to look at the reality of the situation. Most such feelings evaporate when we bring them to our awareness and think about them. If the person you are talking with is still anxious about the other person's reaction, there is probably a need to talk more about their relationship with that person.

EXERCISE NINE: GUILT AND REALISM
(ten minutes)

- A carer feels guilty because they feel they are not doing enough. They feel guilty for not always being willing and sweet tempered.
- A mother feels guilty for scolding her child, or smacking it.
- A teenage girl feels guilty for having sex with her boyfriend.
- A man feels guilty for killing someone in a drink drive accident.
- A parent feels guilty because their child died in the car accident.

Think of these cases. Do you think the people concerned are guilty?

What would help them move forward?

Can you feel fellow feeling for them?

Imagine people coming to you to talk about one of these situations. How would you feel? Would you feel able to support them? Would you feel judgemental towards them?

Think of real situations which you have experienced of people who felt guilty and talked to you about it.

Session Ten

Working with Grief & Loss

This session will include:

- Varieties of loss
- Complicated loss
- Impermanence
- Facing the reality of loss
- Identity and loss
- Supporting people through experiences of loss
- The grief process

A World of Losses

When we think of loss we probably immediately think of bereavement. The death of a loved one is such a big event, creating a huge hole in one's personal world. It is bound to impact on our lives in big ways. But bereavement can wear many clothes. Quite apart from the infinite variations in human reaction, and in the nature of relationships, the actual death itself might have happened in a whole variety of ways, each of which will affect how it is experienced. A death can be expected or sudden, timely or untimely, resulting from illness or accident. These differences affect how we experience the loss.

When we speak of loss, however, we are not only talking about deaths. Loss takes other forms too. In one sense, we can view every life event as a loss. For anything new to happen, something else ceases. For every gain, there is a loss. For every change, something must be let go. When we look at loss in this way, we start to see life as an ever shifting territory in which nothing is fixed or stable.

Mostly, though, it is the more serious losses which we are

thinking about in this session. Ordinary, every day loses are mostly passed over without big reaction, though they may affect us in small ways. More substantive losses break into the ordinary pattern of life and change its course. They force us to reassess what we are doing. Such losses might include things like: losing a job, moving house, becoming disabled, falling out with a friend, having one's child leave home, failing an exam, not succeeding in getting onto a course, divorcing and many other things.

If you look at a list which rates life-stress factors, you will find that most of the events listed in the previous paragraph are on it. Indeed, as one looks down such a list, most, if not all, of the items on it involve a strong element of loss. Loss is stressful. This stress is partly to do with the pain involved in losing something we cherish but it is also to do with the disruption which the loss causes to our personal world. Loss and bereavement affect not only our emotions, but also our sense of who we are.

Some losses are severe and some are less so. Some are sudden and others gradual. Some involve things we have some control over and maybe even choose, whilst others are imposed upon us. The amount of preparation which we have in each case, and the level of choice involved in such changes, affects our experience. They may help us to integrate the loss into our world view and to feel some control over the situation. Nevertheless, any major loss has impact, even if it is foreseen and prepared for.

As listeners, we will find that many of the people who come to talk to us will have experienced major loss. Often, it is the disruption which a bereavement or life change causes which precipitates someone to seek out help.

EXERCISE ONE: VARIETIES OF LOSS
(fifteen minutes)

Think of somebody whom you are supporting, or perhaps someone who you know personally. It needs to be somebody you know fairly well. Make a list of all the experiences of loss which that person has experienced over the last year. You can do this simply by making a listing or you could mark them onto a time line or calendar.

Notice which losses you thought of first. Were these the most obvious ones? Were they the ones which the other person found most difficult to handle? Have they stuck in your mind for other reasons?

Did you identify losses which you hadn't previously been aware of?

How do you think the losses affected the person emotionally? Were there good feelings involved as well as bad ones?

The Reality of Loss

Grief and loss are very significant factors in forming our psychological states. Change is everywhere and loss is an inevitable part of life. Even pleasurable things come to an end, so relying on being able to distract ourselves with positive thoughts or pleasant activities when things go wrong is liable to let us down in the end.

Loss is not something which we can avoid, yet too often it becomes a source of shame or evasion. It is challenging to face the reality of what has happened, to accept and experience the feelings which arise as a result, and to work through them and integrate them. Yet loss is part of life and not something to be hidden away or to cause embarrassment.

An important step in facing loss is to recognise the truth of what has happened. The person has died, or the relationship has ended, or the car has been written off. If we do this, we will not be tying up a lot of psychological energy in denial. Instead, we can harness that energy and use it to get our lives back on course instead of shying away from it and trying to suppress it.

More than this, though, the experience of loss itself generates a lot of emotional energy. Initially, this is most appropriately expressed in grief, but later, as the acute grief subsides, some people will direct this energy into worthwhile action. We have all known people who, after a death, have suddenly found a new cause or a sense of purpose and have become more effective, happier and fulfilled as a result.

Loss is a reality which we need not feel that we need to run away from, and yet time and again we do.

- On the one hand we tend to avoid the reality of the many losses which occur in life. (In the next session we will look at how compulsive, clinging and addictive patterns are typical of the ways we avoid the reality of losses.)
- On the other hand, if we can face the reality of our situation we will live healthier lives. We will be more in touch with the good things in life as well as the hard ones.

Objects and Reminders

After a major loss, the feeling of grief is pervasive and, for the person who is grieving, the ebb and flow of emotions is constantly being triggered by reminders in everyday life.

Many of these reminders are embedded in the physical environment which was once the shared space of the relationship.

The bereaved person is surrounded by objects, each of which holds the memories of a long companionship. Finding such items both creates a link with the person who has died, and brings fresh evidence of the loss. The surviving partner comes across a favourite book, an article of clothing, a walking stick, and, seeing them, is filled with tears. Sometimes a person who has been bereaved may feel so upset that they cannot bear to look at certain things or to go through the dead person's possessions. They may feel disloyal giving things away, or simply that they cannot bear to part with them.

As we have seen, objects can provide a potent connection with loved ones who are absent. Sometimes the bereaved person may carry a personal item as a way of feeling close to the person who has died. Susan keeps her mother's photograph in her purse. Tony carries his son's commemorative medal. Fazal uses his grandmother's embroidered cloth to cover a shelf in his living room.

As a listener, you may be able to support the person by reassuring them that it is quite normal to have such objects which support the feeling of connection with the loved one, encouraging them to go through the processes of grieving at their own pace, and sharing with them in honouring the memories which such possessions contain.

Compounded Losses

When we experience a major loss, one of the things which may make it difficult to handle is that there are often a lot of smaller losses associated with the main loss. For example, if a person moves house, they not only lose their old home, but they are often further from friends, they may lose things they enjoyed such as a view or a garden, they may have a different journey to work, or have to change jobs and so on. Moving house might be something which they looked forward to, but some of the secondary loses might be surprising and in some cases upsetting.

With a major bereavement, the secondary losses can be huge. Not only is the loved one lost, but also the person who drove the car or changed the fuses or cooked the dinner or earned the main family income, as well as the person who helped with the Sunday crossword and shared trips to the cinema. Such practical losses can be particularly painful as they are reminders of the shared life which has gone. With each of them, the reality of the death becomes more certain.

Many of the secondary losses are connected with a person's sense of identity. They no longer have the status of husband or wife, son or daughter. Attributes of the previous role are lost with the end of a relationship or the death of a partner.

Whether the loss comes about through bereavement or through some other change of situation, one of the things which you might offer to someone who has experienced such a major loss is a space in which to recognise some of the secondary losses and appreciate their impact.

EXERCISE TWO: IDENTIFYING SECONDARY LOSSES

(five minutes)

Take one of the bigger losses which you identified in exercise one. Write down a word or sentence which describes this loss in the middle of a piece of paper.

Now think of secondary losses which the person experienced, associated with this primary loss. Write words to describe these subsidiary losses on the page arranged around the primary loss, then link them with lines to the primary loss, and if appropriate to each other, creating a net diagram.

You may find, as you record these, that there is a third level of loss which arose from some of these secondary losses. For example, a partner's death might have led to the person moving house, which might have led to losses of friends, favourite walks, a view over the park and so on.

Think about how these different losses impacted upon the person.

Were they aware of them at the time? Were the losses overshadowed by the primary loss? How did they deal with them?

If you were the person who experienced these losses, what effect do you think identifying the secondary losses would have had on you?

Sometimes a person may come to talk with you because they are uncomfortable about their feelings. Perhaps they find they are ambivalent about something which they felt they should be looking forward to, such as a new job or a wedding. In such a situation, it can be especially helpful to talk about the possibility that other losses might be involved. Feeling ambivalent about such an event can be distressing and anxiety provoking. The person starts to doubt the decision they have made, but really the feelings of ambivalence may come from the things which are being given up, rather than the job or the wedding itself.

In such cases, simply recognising that there are feelings of loss arising from the secondary effects of the change, which exist alongside the more positive ones related to the main event, can be enough to reassure. Identifying such factors can help a person to work out what they need to do to re-establish their equilibrium –

maybe finding something that will replace the thing which is missed.

EXERCISE THREE: SUSAN'S STORY
(twenty minutes)

Susan is about to marry Tom and join him in Australia where he is working. Initially she was very excited about the new life, but now that the wedding is approaching, she has started having nightmares and feels sick when she thinks about getting on the plane after the wedding. Although she loves Tom, she is beginning to wonder if she has made the right decision.

Imagine that you are Susan and have gone to talk things over with a listener. What would you hope the listener could offer you?

Imagine that after you had spoken with the listener, you wrote down your thoughts. What would you write? *(Write for ten minutes as Susan)*

Now stop imagining yourself in Susan's shoes and imagine yourself as the listener. Reflect on how you, as a listener, would have handled the conversation.

Chronic and Cumulative Loss

Some losses happen over time. This can go unrecognised, but the loss may still eat away at that person's spirit. Whilst a sudden loss is acute and painful, a chronic loss may not even be thought of as such. Without acknowledgement, the slow diminishment of faculties or resources, which the loss involves, may lead to depression.

As a listener, you are likely to be involved with people who have experienced, or are experiencing, chronic or cumulative losses. The elderly, for example, face losses of health and fitness, as well as of lifestyle, income, looks, loved ones, mobility, and so are particularly vulnerable to depression. This, in turn, is often not diagnosed because symptoms such as slowness or confusion, which may be linked to depression, are often put down to age and not taken seriously. By showing appreciation for the person, who still feels just as they did at twenty, but is forced into a limited lifestyle by an ailing body, you may help that person express some of the sadness which comes from such losses.

People with disabilities also experience many losses. Some will have lost faculties through degenerative illness. Supporting a person who knows that their health and capacity to do things will deteriorate over time is not easy. A person in this position may not only feel the loss of lifestyle and mobility which they have already experienced, but also grieve in anticipation of what is to come. Others may have become disabled suddenly in accidents or had disabilities from birth. In addition to the restrictions which any disability brings, they may experience a sense of other lives which might have been, had the accident not occurred, or had they been born without the disability. Among the intangibles may lurk a feeling of having lost a future, particularly if the disability is getting worse. It is easy for such a person to become fiercely positive and brave, and as a listener, you may be impressed and supportive of such an attitude, but it may also be important to give space for the other voice, and allow the person to talk about the times when everything seems too much and despair takes over. As listener, it can be very helpful, if you are able, to hold both sides of the situation for the person. You might say something like, "It's just amazing how much you manage to do and how positive you always are, and I guess there are also some times when you must get overwhelmed by it all. We all have bad days, and sometimes it is good to talk about it."

People whose living situation is poor, through being refugees or long term unemployed, or for some other reason, may experience a chronic sense of loss arising from the loss of hopes, specific or general, as well as from particular deprivations. For someone who was not born in their present country of residence, there may be a longing for the homeland, and for those left behind, even when returning would be dangerous or impossible.

EXERCISE FOUR: MALCOLM'S STORY
(twenty minutes)

Malcolm worked in a factory for thirty-five years until it closed and left him redundant at the age of fifty-three. With very little redundancy money and no prospect of finding another job, Malcolm saw his savings gradually dwindling. Holiday times came round but he no longer had money to go away. Christmas came and went, but as he lived on his own, without his mates from the factory, there was no one to celebrate with. His car developed problems and he could not afford to replace it. Malcolm became increasingly isolated, unhappy and depressed.

Imagine that you are Malcolm. One day you call into the community centre which is close to your house. You have not been there before, but are walking past and wonder if there might be something for you to get involved in. A community worker approaches you.

What would you hope the worker could offer you?

Imagine that the worker asks you about your life, what will you say and what will you not say? What would help you to face the changes which have happened in your life? What else do you need? (Write for ten minutes, as Malcolm, about your situation)

Now reflect on how you would have handled the conversation if you had been the community worker. How could you have invited Malcolm to talk about his problems?

EXERCISE FIVE: EXPLORING CHRONIC LOSS
(twenty-five minutes)

Think of a person whom you have worked with or know well who suffers from major cumulative or chronic loss.

Imagine that you are that person. Write for fifteen minutes without stopping, recording the different losses that you have experienced, and what it is like to be in your situation. Record how it has changed over time and whether you see it changing in the future.

Stop writing and re-read what you have read. If you were in a listener role in relation to this person, what help could you offer?

Think yourself back into role as the other person to see how your answer feels.

Then reflect on your learning from this exercise.

Impermanence

Everything is impermanent. All things are of the nature to change. We live in a situation of flux, and in this we face loss in every moment.

At the same time, impermanence is the rich fabric from which life constantly re-creates itself. Moment by moment, new opportunities arise, as space is created by the departing old.

To some extent, the way that we see loss is a matter of habit. If we are constantly looking back at the past, we may be much more conscious of what has been lost than we are of the new opportunities. We may be filled with regret and feel depressed. If we constantly look forward, we may be less caught up with such things, but we may also be inclined to deny serious losses which need to be mourned. Doing this may not be healthy either.

The habits, which we have acquired over a lifetime, are often created by our earlier experiences. In this way, a person who experienced a lot of loss in childhood, or who grew up in a family which looked on the negative side of life, may be more likely to lean towards seeing life as a series of losses. Not all habits are created in childhood though. A person who has had a series of bereavements in recent years may equally have come to expect that the next is only just around the corner.

So there is probably a balance to be struck: a time to mourn and a time to be happy, a time for tears and a time to put grief aside and get on with life.

Identity and Loss

We have already seen how our sense of identity is closely tied up with the important people, things and places in our lives. In our familiar environments, the things around us reflect who we think we are. We choose things which are 'my kind of thing'. These things, in turn, shape us.

This is partly because we create our environments in ways which reflect our tastes; we furnish our houses and select other possessions, such as clothes or cars or even our workplaces, to fit our personal preferences, or to demonstrate to other people our sense of who we are. (Sometimes a person with a negative image of themselves might choose drab clothes or a poorly paid job.)

Also, we start to identify with the things which are familiar and to feel ourselves reflected in the places and things which we see or use every day. They may not be our personal possessions, but we still feel them to, in some way, be ours.

In addition to this, when we look at the world around us, we tend to notice the things which interest us and not to see those which do not. We may even misinterpret things which we see. This process of seeing things selectively biases our world view. We see things which reflect a sense of 'how it is' and 'how I am'.

All of this means that when a significant thing is removed from our world, that item ceases to be a mirror for us. Our sense of self depends on having a world which reflects who we think we are. When that world changes, there can be a loss of identity.

So, in quite concrete ways, our identity is threatened by losses. A woman cannot cling to her identity as a mother once her child has grown up, (though of course, she may find new ways to develop the role as a grandmother or as a confidante.) A man cannot be the school teacher once he has retired; he becomes another person in the pension queue. A wife loses her identity as wife when her husband dies; she has to learn how to be a widow.

Our sense of self is closely tied in with the world we inhabit, so any loss in that world affects our sense of who we are. At the same time, our sense of self is basically a defensive mechanism. It is one of the ways that we create some illusion of permanence in the ever shifting situation. We think of our selves as a constant, unchanging phenomenon.

Thus, a major loss can precipitate a feeling of losing identity, just at the time when we most need that defence of feeling that we know who we are and where we are going in life. The loss becomes a double loss. We feel the pain of losing the loved one or the job or the home or our health, and alongside it we lose the sense of identity which usually gives us the stability of mind to cope with crises. It is not easy.

EXERCISE SIX: LOSS AND IDENTITY
(ten minutes)

Recall the situation of loss which you explored in exercise one. Do you think this loss affected the person's sense of identity? If so, how? What effect did this have on their ability to cope with the loss?

Think about experiences of loss which you have faced. How have these impacted upon your identity?

Are there things which you can learn from your own experience or that of people whom you have known, which will help you to support others who are facing major losses?

Supporting Someone at a Time of Loss

In addition to all these psychological factors, the social context in which people live may make it difficult for them to find support at the time of bereavement. The person who is recently bereaved is often isolated. Other people may find it hard to listen to their painful feelings and may shy away from talking with them.

Sometimes people find it difficult to face another person's grief because they have unresolved feelings of grief themselves. Other people's experiences of loss may evoke feelings about losses that were experienced in the past, so people may be reluctant to be reminded of death. After the First World War, people in Britain often avoided talking about death or bereavement because so many people had lost husbands or sons. It was just too painful. People got used to not discussing feelings of grief, and to changing the subject when someone seemed likely to get emotional. To some extent this pattern has persisted, particularly among older people.

Often, though, the reluctance to approach someone who has recently been bereaved comes out of concern. We are afraid of intruding, perhaps feeling that we did not know the person who died well enough. People often feel that they do not know what to say. Pleasantries seem inappropriate, but to refer immediately to the loss seems too direct. In this, as a listener, it is worth having a few phrases in mind which you can use to broach such a conversation. Although these may feel slightly artificial, once the ice has been broken, the bereaved person will usually be glad to talk and things will flow spontaneously. Something simple like "I'm really sorry," or "How's it going?" or "I've been thinking of you," can be helpful as openers. It is as well to avoid cliché in your phrasing or tone, but even if your response feels a bit clumsy, it is likely to be better than ignoring the person because you don't know what to say.

Another fear which people have in approaching a recently bereaved person is that they will upset the person. If you ask somebody who has just lost a loved one how things are going, they might burst into tears. In practice, this need not be a problem, though. If the person is someone who is likely to be embarrassed, and you are in a very public space, it may be better to wait until you are somewhere a bit more private before inviting such conversation, but more often than not the bereaved person's need to talk and to cry is sufficient, and the grief so natural, that they are unconcerned about being seen in tears. It is more often the listener who feels the embarrassment. Tears are a natural and healthy part of grieving, and having someone to cry with is important to many people in those early days after a death.

FACING OUR OWN LOSSES

To be able to support other people who are grieving, it is valuable to be able to face our own experiences. To help others, we need to have digested losses which have happened to us and also to have looked at our own fears about death and loss. If we are able to do this we will be less likely to evade other people's grief. When our own grief is raw, we may not be ready to offer support to others. Later, we may find that drawing on our experience helps us to offer fellow feeling to the newly bereaved, but when we are in the midst of emotion ourselves, it is unlikely we will be able to listen well to others.

EXERCISE SEVEN: FACING YOUR OWN LOSSES
(ten minutes)

Reflect back over your life and make a list of twelve losses which you have experienced. These might be bereavements but might include other losses.

Rate the losses on a seismic scale of one to ten. How big an earthquake did each loss cause in your life?

Now look at what you needed in each case in order to work through your feelings. How long did the acute phase of grief or pain last? What sort of feelings are still with you?

How are the feelings which you are left with related to the sort of help which you received at the time of the loss?

The Process of Grieving

There are a number of models which describe the process which a person goes through as they come to terms with bereavement or other major loss. The best known of these models are probably those which are presented in the works of Elizabeth Kubler-Ross, Peter Marris and William Worden. If you are working with the dying or with bereaved people, do become familiar with these important books since they offer much more detailed suggestions for working with people in such situations than there is space for here.

All these writers present models of the grieving process, and suggest that a bereaved person goes through a series of stages in resolving the grief. Their models differ slightly from one another, emphasising different aspects of the dying and bereavement process, but broadly they follow similar patterns.

From these models, one can conclude that certain tasks need to be gone through after bereavement. The model which is presented below is grounded in similar principles, and is based on the model presented in a paper by Leick & Davidsen-Nielsen called *The Four Tasks of Griefwork.* (This is published in Stoner's book, *Attachment Loss and Grief Therapy*, published by Routledge). As might be supposed, this paper sets out four tasks.

When we talk about 'tasks' of grieving, the intention is not to tell a grieving person what they must do. This list of 'tasks' is really a description of natural occurrences that unfold as the person goes through stages in the mourning processes.

The model is helpful in two respects. Firstly it is supportive to the person who is grieving, who may feel that their emotions are out of control and that they are becoming chaotic and confused. It is reassuring to be able to see that the feelings are simply what are to be expected at this stage.

Secondly, the model may be helpful if you are supporting the grieving person and suspect that the person is not moving through the grief in a normal way. It may give some indication of what aspect of the grief is not being looked at or experienced. In this way, you may be able to gently encourage the person to look at something which they are avoiding.

The four tasks of grieving, which Leick & Davidsen-Nielsen identify, usually follow, roughly, in the order which they are presented, but they may not necessarily follow in a tidy way. The person may backtrack from time to time. The tasks are:

- **Accepting reality**: After a death, or other major loss, people can feel numb, disbelieving, and disorientated. They may keep finding themselves acting as if the dead person were still around, and life hadn't changed. They may even experience the person's presence, or think they see them in familiar places. They may find it hard to make changes, such as giving away the person's possessions or even moving them. At this stage, your role as listener is one of support. It may also be one of gently encouraging the person to talk about the person who has died. In particular, you might talk about the events leading up to the death and the death itself.

- **Entering emotions of grief**: Once the reality of the loss becomes apparent, the person is likely to go through a lot of emotions. These may include anger and sadness, despair and guilt. Emotions may swing from one extreme to another and the person often moves in and out of denial and strong feelings. They may have short periods of what seems like numbness, but in the circumstances, this is perfectly normal and will pass. During this phase, your continuing support will provide a steady presence during the swings of emotion. You might need to give reassurance that feelings of anger or low mood are part of the process of grief, and will pass. You might also encourage the person to recall the loved one who has died and invite them to tell you about their story. You could begin by asking about things which were associated with the dead person, like photographs or possessions. If you are in the person's home, there may be many reminders around in the room that carry poignant stories.

- **Learning new skills**: Gradually, as the emotional storm subsides, the person starts to learn to cope on their own in the new circumstances. This can involve learning in practical ways. For example, it may mean learning to cook, mend the car or fill in tax forms. Learning new emotional and social skills is also important. For example, where a couple were used to socialising together, the remaining partner may need to learn to go out alone. At this stage, your support may be practical, but don't be in too much of a rush to move on from the stage of expressing feelings. Moving on will involve encountering many secondary losses as the bereaved person realises once again that their loved one really has died. This may also be a time when you can help the person to create some sort of ongoing memorial for the person who died.

- **Reinvesting energy**: As the bereaved person moves on, the energy, which was taken up with grieving, needs to be used in new ways. The grief process may end in a positive phase of exploration and creativity in which the loved one is not forgotten, but their memory becomes a support for the new life rather than a barrier to it. This does not mean that periods of sadness cease. They may recur any time, but they become less frequent and less acute as time goes on. In this stage your role may be to draw back. If you have been supporting the bereaved person throughout the process, it is probably time to let go, and this may involve a smaller experience of grief and loss. Give time to acknowledge these feelings.

PROBLEMS IN THE GRIEVING PROCESS

Grief is usually a natural process which unfolds over time. Sometimes, however, it becomes problematic because the person gets stuck in one phase. This can happen particularly when personal circumstances around a death are complicated and evoke mixed feelings.

Perhaps there was some relief when the death came because caring for the person who died was difficult. Perhaps the relationship was strained or ambivalent. Perhaps more than one death happened at once, as in a bad car accident. Perhaps the bereaved person had to 'stay strong' for others. When emotions are mixed in such ways, grief can be delayed or avoided, but then cause problematic mental or physical symptoms later, or it can become chronic and fail to resolve or to lose intensity.

EXERCISE EIGHT: THE TASKS OF GRIEVING
(five minutes)

Look at the tasks of grieving set out above and compare them with the experiences which you identified in exercise seven.

Do you recognise these stages in your own experiences of grief?

Did you experience the tasks unfolding in the order which the model suggests or did something else happen?

If you were to make your own model based on your own experience, what stages would you include?

Take each of the four tasks in turn and make notes on what role you think the listener might take in supporting people in this stage of grief.

An Anchor in Reality

When we sit with someone who has just lost the person they loved most in all the world, the gulf between us and them can feel as wide as an ocean. How can we reach out and find them? How can we offer a hand to hold, and an ear to listen? Our words seem to echo, crass and cold, in the gaping emptiness of their grief. Yet being there, we are perhaps the only spark of life on a barren horizon.

In the aftermath of bereavement, people are often very much wrapped up in their own thoughts and feelings and with memories of the person who has died. This is normal. Grief weaves a cocoon of sadness around the person so that their involvement with the world becomes minimal and mechanical. Their real interest may be entirely caught up in the other world of the dead. In the time immediately after a death, this withdrawal is normal, but in the weeks and months that follow, the person needs to gradually find there way back to the world of the living.

In this process, you, as listener, can play an important role by acting as a link to the ordinary world. As we have already seen, people's connections with other people are particularly important in preventing them from becoming completely lost in private worlds and limited perspectives. The presence of others and their loving contact gently challenges the person to communicate and brings him into contact with reality. So, you become an anchor for the bereaved person. This anchor can be a lifeline. The two-way communication restores the person's faith in life.

Occasionally this lifeline may be literal, for sometimes the bereaved person feels little reason to go on living, especially where they have no other family or support. The pull toward the world of the dead person is so strong, that they slip into thinking of joining them. So, on rare occasions, the bereaved person becomes suicidal. If the person you are supporting seems suicidal and you suspect such thoughts may be acted on, talk with your supervisor or manager urgently about your worries, and encourage the person to seek more help, maybe through their doctor.

Mostly, though, such thoughts are fleeting and not acted upon. The regular, caring presence of a listener is important for the comfort which it brings. Time seems unbearably drawn out in those early weeks, and days pass slowly. The regular visit and the friendly cup of tea which is shared give meaning in the moment by moment negotiation of a barren world.

Helping the Person Experiencing Grief

The person who has recently suffered a loss, whether through bereavement or other life changes, often looks to others for support. There may be a great need to talk, to give space to recall events, and share memories and feelings. Whether the person turns to friends or to a professional counsellor or listener, the companionship is important.

Feelings change a lot, especially in the early days. Sometimes they can be very strong and acutely painful. A person may feel cut off from ordinary life or may report seeing or hearing the dead person. Such experiences are not unusual, and can be very comforting. However strange, in the early days after a death, most such responses are part of the normal grieving process. You may simply need to reassure the person that this is so and that such experiences will pass.

Expression of grief is healthy, but some people grieve more privately than others. People vary in their needs, so be guided by the person you are supporting. If they need to talk about their feelings, encourage them, but if they prefer to talk about day to day matters, it may be enough just to say something which acknowledges the unspoken feelings, such as, "It must be hard at the moment. I can see you have a lot of feelings." And then share in talking about the garden or the family.

ADVICE AND ENCOURAGEMENT

The grieving person can be reassured by knowing that what they are going through is normal. When feelings are extreme, a person can feel very alone and may fear they are going mad. It is comforting to know that others have felt similarly and have eventually moved on. It may also be good to reassure the newly bereaved person that there is no need to rush into making changes. Grieving takes time, often years rather than months, and there will come points where personal effects of the deceased can be given away – but not now. Be careful not to press the person into doing practical things before they are ready, unless it is absolutely essential. Take the attitude that you are accompanying the person on their journey, rather than thinking that you are the expert.

CEREMONIES AND MEMORIALS

The funeral service is often seen as the focus for the grieving ritual, but it comes early in the grief process and the bereaved person may still be feeling very numb from the death. Nevertheless, the funeral creates a memory of having marked the death, which can be drawn on in the following months of grieving. It may be quite uplifting, especially if many people attend and give testimony to the person who has died. If you are supporting someone at this time, encourage them to make the funeral as personal as they wish, including favourite readings and reflections, but also, if they are the partner of the person who died, or closely related, encourage them to hand over the main organisation of the event to someone else.

Sometimes other ceremony is also helpful. If there is a later ceremony to scatter ashes or a memorial service, this may be better timed for the bereaved person and may mark a stage in moving on from the initial grief phase. Having an ongoing place of memorial can also be a great comfort. Visiting a grave or site where ashes were scattered can maintain a feeling of intimacy with the dead person.

The bereaved person might also create a focus in the home for remembering the loved one. In some cultures ancestor shrines are normal in every home, and something similar may help people from any background. The memorial might be as simple as a photo on a shelf or a special place associated with the person who died. Such a place can provide a space where the loved one's presence is felt. The bereaved person can return there to be close to the person who has died (but also have a sense of leaving the person behind in a safe space when they go back to everyday life.)

Flowers or other things can be put at the grave or in a memorial place in the home. The impulse to make offerings to the dead has been widespread in human cultures since the dawn of time. Whether in roadside shrines, at the grave or in the home, people feel drawn to mark and give form to their grief by placing gifts and tokens at significant sites. This may have religious meaning for some, but it can also be very comforting to people who have no formal faith.

EXERCISE NINE: CREATING A MEMORIAL SPACE
(twenty minutes)

Create a space within your quiet corner to remember the people you know who have died. This might be a shelf or a small table top. Place on it photographs (or if you do not have any, create a suitable image or object to remind you of the person). Add mementoes, a candle, flowers and anything else you wish in order to create a special focus for your meditation.

Sit quietly for a time facing this space and remember those people whose photographs or images you have assembled. Imagine sending blessings to them.

SUPPORT NETWORKS

Support groups can be helpful to the bereaved person, as can other social networks. Finding new friendships may be an important part of the grieving process.

For some people, being with others can offer support whilst they are in the midst of their grief. It can be comforting to share feelings and see others who have gone through similar feelings. Seeing that people reach a stage of re-engaging with life can be reassuring. For other people, renewed socialising is part of a later phase of grieving.

It is not good to press a person to socialise too early, however. It is a well known phenomenon for people who have been bereaved to fall into inappropriate relationships whilst they are emotionally vulnerable just as people on the rebound from a separation might.

Although loss is painful, grieving can also be a transformational process from which people emerge stronger and more engaged with life. The support which you give a grieving person can help them to face their loss and thus emerge, having grown in maturity and wisdom.

Session Eleven

Compulsion & Addiction

This session will include:

- Compulsive and addictive behaviours as avoidance
- Negative and positive triggers
- Identity and habit patterns
- Habits of speech
- Addiction
- Three stages of attachment

We tend to respond to everyday losses and afflictions by escaping into various distractions. We find things which comfort us or which take our minds off the painful aspects of our lives.

On a day to day level, this is not a problem. If we spent all of our time dwelling on the various things which go wrong in our lives or on the inevitable losses which happen all the time, we would probably have rather grim lives. The sage may spend his days contemplating impermanence, but most of us have not reached the dizzying heights where we do not sometimes need to deliberately introduce a bit of lightness into our lives.

On the other hand, if we are never willing to face reality and are constantly escaping and blocking our feelings through distractions, and by accumulating possessions, our behaviour will start to become driven by our need not to face up to things and thus become compulsive. We may even fall prey to addictions.

So there is a middle line. The healthy position is, for most of us, to be able to face things when we have to, and to be able to look honestly at our lives and our feelings. When we can do this, we are not driven by our need to hide these feelings from ourselves and others. At the same time, we need to be able to put feelings down when this becomes appropriate and to enjoy ourselves or get on with our everyday work. We need not be compulsive about looking at painful feelings. Sometimes we need to be able to distract ourselves and mentally 'change the subject'.

So life becomes a negotiation between facing the reality of the various difficulties which beset us, and our patterns of avoiding this reality. In the last session we looked at how life can involve many painful losses. We looked at the reality factor; the grief and regret which all of us sometimes face. In this session we will look at the escapist aspect of human experience. We will look at the sorts of patterns of distraction, compulsion and addiction which are the other side of the coin of loss. When people cannot face reality, or do not want to acknowledge it, they tend to get into patterns of avoidance.

These patterns are as multi-faceted as human psychology. There is a sense in which all of our mental and behavioural problems can be seen as examples of compulsion or addictive behaviours, but here we will focus on the more obvious examples.

Compulsiveness

Human psychology is often driven by processes of distraction. When we want to distract ourselves, we frequently do so by using something which we enjoy to take our mind off a problem or unpleasant event. This is a normal response, and not problematic at this everyday level, but at the extreme, it can end up in us getting hooked on something and doing it in a compulsive way.

We might do something physical like going for a drink or a watching a favourite television programme, or we might use something psychological as a distraction, like holding on tenaciously to an opinion or minor worry. At the ordinary level, these things provide a temporary amusement or distraction, but if they become compulsive, they can become something which drives us and stops us thinking clearly or relating to others properly.

Compulsion builds up over time. Initially we simply occupy our senses with something which is compelling for us. We reach for something pleasant, comforting or exciting to take our mind off unpleasant thoughts or feelings which are coming up in us. This sort of pleasant distraction is the commonest. Sometimes, though, we use something which is physically painful to distract ourselves. This is more likely if we are really stressed or upset. For example we might clench our hands till the nails cut into our palms.

We all have a variety of habitual ways of distracting ourselves. These might include things like food, drink, television, sports or sometimes painful things like biting our nails. Most of these things are not a problem because we use them in moderation. They help us regulate our emotional responses and create breaks when they are too intense.

EXERCISE ONE: DISTRACTIONS
(five minutes)

Think about ways in which you take your mind off stressful or painful situations?

What do you do when you get in after a bad day? Do you have a favourite food or drink, take a bath, watch television?

Write about your personal pattern of dealing with unpleasant feelings.

These distractions, however, tend to get repeated. Once we have found a distraction that works for us, we tend to repeat it over and over. It becomes a habit. It also becomes something we find ourselves wanting to do for its own sake. This is when we might start to think of it as a compulsion.

We can think of compulsions as being of three kinds:
- *Attractive* compulsions, which involve getting hooked on things or clinging onto them. An attractive compulsion is one where we want something or use it repeatedly, for example particular foods or drink or an exercise routine.

- *Aversive* compulsions involve negative relationships with things. We compulsively push them away, yet still cannot get them out of our heads. For example, the person who always reads the daily paper and rants about the government or immigration may be caught in an aversive compulsion. Likewise, someone who is anorexic might be said to have an aversive relationship with food; they are constantly thinking of it and obsessed with it, but push it away.

- *Complex* compulsions are to things with which we have a confused relationship. These involve the ambivalent and love-hate responses which we have to things. We do not know if we want them or do not want them, but we cannot let them go either.

As we repeat our various patterns of distraction, we also start to become identified with them. Our identity is really made up of our habitual ways of acting and thinking, so is closely connected with the way that we distract ourselves when we are under pressure. So, although we would not describe everything which we enjoy or feel connected to as compulsive by any means, there is a link between identification and compulsion.

Understanding that attachment can be positive or negative, and seeing its function in establishing our sense of identity and protecting us from psychological pain, can help us to appreciate why people may be so strong in asserting their views or hanging onto things which they like to do.

Everyday Distractions

Many of the ordinary things which we do every day provide minor distractions for us. Of course most of these things are harmless, and many are good things to do in themselves. The fact that we use an activity as a way of distracting ourselves from things that we are unhappy or anxious about does not necessarily make it a bad thing to do. Going to a football match might take our minds off problems we have at home and is also an enjoyable activity. Going out for a meal or for drinks with friends might distract us from stresses at work, but it also strengthens our friendships and gives us an evening of stimulating conversation. Also, whilst an ideal might be to take everything which life throws at us in our stride, the reality is that, as humans, we often need a break from stressful situations.

EXERCISE TWO: DIARY EXERCISE ON DISTRACTIONS
(indeterminate)

Keep a diary over a week, writing in it at least twice a day (midday and evening ideally.)

Rule the diary in two columns and in one column record things which you noticed yourself doing or thinking which might be being used, at least in part, as a distraction. In the other column record what you are distracting yourself from.

At the end of the week read back over the diary and see what sorts of things you have recorded. Are there things which surprise you or patterns of behaviour which you would not have been aware of?

Annotate your diary, commenting on these observations and on whether there are behaviours you would like to change.

You might like to repeat this exercise over a shorter period of time, for example a morning, keeping the diary beside you and noting every impulse to distract yourself as it happens, and what preceded it. This can be particularly useful if you are trying to break a habit like compulsive eating or smoking.

The people who you are supporting are probably suffering in some way, and they will have their ways of coping with the feelings which this brings up. It may be that the ways they get through are positive or it may be that they are more problematic. If a person is avoiding feelings by excessive drinking or endless computer games, for example, you may be able to encourage them to talk more about the issues which are troubling them.

Depending on how 'hooked' the person is, this may be helpful. You may also be able to help them find other ways of coping. Learning grounding or relaxation methods can be very helpful in this respect, as they provide good ways of interrupting unhappy thoughts and providing positive balance in a person's life.

EXERCISE THREE: COPING STRATEGIES
(five minutes)

Think about someone whom you have been working with or supporting. What methods or things do they use to help them to cope with the stresses in their life? Make a list.

Now take a sheet of paper and divide it into three columns. In the first column, write down the list of behaviours. In the second column write down the advantages of the behaviour, and in the third column write down the disadvantages.

Are some of the behaviours basically unhelpful? Can you think of things which you might suggest or do to help the person cope better and give them strategies which they could use when they are on their own?

Becoming Compulsive

We distract ourselves in all kinds of ways when we feel stressed or overwhelmed. This is not necessarily unhealthy. Problems arise where the behaviour becomes compulsive. Going for a run is a healthy thing to do, but if a person has reached the stage where they are refusing invitations to go out with friends or becoming anxious if they are unable to get out jogging, it becomes something that drives their life rather than being a pleasure. Then it ceases to be helpful and starts to become a problem in itself.

We have all met people who get into states of high anxiety when they cannot fit in their daily routines, whether it is some sort of exercise schedule or a particular eating pattern or whatever. Often, it seems as if the stress which the activity was set up to combat has taken over the activity itself. Something else is needed.

Any of us can start to feel this way at times of particular stress. We might do a variety of things compulsively or get 'hooked' on one. If this phase passes quickly, we will probably find ourselves returning to a normal equilibrium, but for some people the compulsiveness becomes established.

EXERCISE FOUR: STRESS AND COMPULSIVENESS
(five minutes)

Think about times when you have felt stressed. Have you ever felt that you got into compulsive patterns of behaviour? If so, has this worried you?

Have you known other people who have responded to pressure with compulsive behaviours? How did you respond?

Reflect on your observations, whether of yourself or someone else under stress. Do they help you to understand people whom you are working with better? Do they give you clues about how you might respond to them?

Anchors, Distractions and Distress

Your presence as a listener can provide an anchor for the person who is extremely distressed. It can hold them in contact with real world when their chaotic thoughts and feelings threaten to engulf them. It anchors them in relationship and provides a life line.

We saw in session five how you can create a symbolic object, such as a stone or other small item, which can be held by the person who is very distressed and carried away with them when they leave your presence.

When somebody is so distressed that they are unable to face life without a constant background noise of distractions, it can be helpful to teach them grounding exercises which use objects as their focus of attention, as opposed to body sensation. These take the person's attention away from the centre of the body, where emotions are felt most keenly, and into the hands and feet which are in contact with the physical world.

Invite the person to hold the anchor stone and to focus their attention on the feeling of it in the palm of their hand. Ask them to explore its texture with their finger tips. In this way, their attention is grounded. They can learn to focus their attention like this whenever they feel stressed.

You might also now like to look back at the section on containment at the end of session five. Offering methods of containment to the people we are working with may be helpful both as an immediate way of supporting them in managing their anxiety and in giving them skills which they can use on other occasions.

Identity and Habit Patterns

People have their typical ways of coping with life. As we build up a personal pattern of distractions and coping behaviours, we also identify with them. Our sense of self is based on our habits. Our sense of identity also colours the way we see the world. In other words, because our sense of self relies upon us finding certain conditions in our immediate surroundings, we have expectations and go out looking for things which reinforce our sense of who we are and how the world is. We look at everything that we encounter with a degree of bias and distortion. We react to the world in ways which are conditioned by our expectations. This in turn reinforces our sense of identity. In this way, we create a cycle in which we go out looking for things which reinforce our sense of who we are.

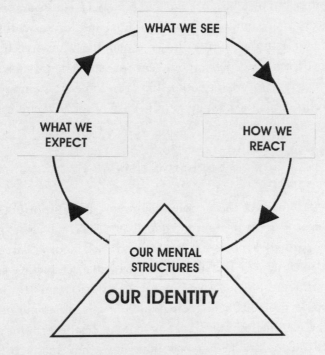

Often the things which are important in maintaining our sense of self are things which we use in some way to distract ourselves from painful aspects of life.

Our sense of self gives us a feeling of permanence and predictability in an unpredictable world, but also it is associated with our coping strategies and the attachments which we have. For these reasons, it is something which we cling to because it helps us to get through anxious times. Things which threaten our sense of self can be particularly scary because they not only threaten what we identify with, but they also threaten to put us back in touch with the various kinds of affliction which caused us to try to escape in the first place.

The problem is that, as we have already seen, many of the worst things that happen to us involve changes which upset our sense of who we are. As we have seen, bereavement, for example, shakes our foundations, not just because of the grief associated with the loss, but also because we lose our social status and sense of identity. We are no longer a wife or husband, but a widow or widower, for example. Other life crises similarly involve things which, by their nature, disrupt our sense of self. When we lose our job, or move house, end a relationship or become sick, among the other implications, the change to our sense of who we are can be very painful.

People in Crisis

As a listener, most of the people whom you are supporting will have a lot of sources of pain in their lives. They may be experiencing a particular crisis or may be in an ongoing stressful situation. In either case it is likely that they will already have some coping strategies. They will naturally find ways to keep themselves distracted from their situation, at least some of the time. These strategies may or may not be healthy. It may be helpful to talk with the person about how they manage their stress. Are there things which help them get through the day or new ways they have found to tackle the situation? These practical things can be very helpful, not just in the changes they bring about, but also in the sense of purpose which they introduce.

It is also worth reflecting on the way that their identity may have been affected by events. Old aspects may have disappeared, but a new identity may be emerging. Supporting this and creating a positive sense of self can be helpful to the person who feels overwhelmed by circumstances. You may help the person to look at what sort of identity they already feel that their role gives them. For example, a carer may have a positive self image, seeing herself as a kind person, or a negative one, seeing herself as a useless victim. Helping the person to identify with the more positive self view can be valuable, especially if this will lead them to become more outgoing and sociable.

Habits of Speech and Repeating Stories

Compulsiveness is expressed in behaviours. People might have habits of action, or of thought. Sometimes a person will have a habitual way of seeing things. They may have a negative view of particular people or the world in general. They may blame themselves or others. They may have stories they tell repeatedly to illustrate their world view.

Thus, one way in which people act compulsively is through their habitual ways of talking. When a person sees the world in a negative way, they speak negatively about it. You may find that some people who come to talk with you have very negative stories about the world and the people around them. If so, you may be able to encourage them to see things differently or to tell their story in a different way. Ask questions. "Is that really true?" "Why do you think she said that?" "What happened to you yesterday that was nice?" Such questions can help the person to shift out of the rut which they have created and gently invite them to experiment with a different world view.

People may also use telling a distressing story as a distraction. This can be confusing, as one can think at first that, in talking about their situation and expressing emotion, the person is really facing their loss or disappointment. The problem is that, because telling the story involves expressing a lot of feeling, this itself can become a feeling distraction and expressing emotion in this habitual way can be a means of diffusing other more deeply held feelings.

We can see an example of how people use emotion to distract themselves from other sadness in their lives if we think about how many people like to go to the cinema to watch weepy films. The emotion they experience is at one remove from their own troubles. At the end of the film the person can walk out of the cinema having had a cathartic experience, without having had to face their own situation directly. This is not a bad thing in itself, but if a person always seeks out indirect ways of exploring emotion, it can be problematic.

Also, in particular as listeners, we need to be careful that our own emotional needs are not being met vicariously through our support of others.

A person who tells their story compulsively may be operating in a similar way. The person talks about events with great emotion, but a part of them is distanced from the reality. The emotional wave, which the repetitious story telling involves, provides a distraction which washes over real engagement with the story.

In such a situation, you may need to support the person in pausing in their account and looking more deeply at what they are saying. If you simply listen to the story again and again in the same way, you may just be encouraging the person to stay stuck in their habit. Getting a new perspective or encouraging them to stop and allow the feelings they are expressing to catch up may shift the compulsion.

Other times, the story may be a distraction from an unspoken fear. The person who compulsively tells a story of their past may be afraid of facing something in their present. They may, for example, be afraid of the responsibilities they would have to take on if they were to get 'better'. They may be afraid of knowing that they are capable of doing more in their life.

EXERCISE SIX: COMPULSIVE STORIES
(five minutes)

Reflect on people you have known who seemed to talk compulsively. What do you think lay behind their compulsion to talk? What effect did it have on their relationships with other people? Did you have a sense of how to help them?

Addiction

When a person is caught in endlessly repeating one particular compulsive behaviour pattern, we often call this an addiction. An addiction can be a physiological dependency in which the body craves a substance such as nicotine, alcohol or other drugs, or it can be a strong psychological attachment which drives the person to repeat the same behaviour. In many addictions there are both physiological and psychological elements.

Addictive patterns are closely tied in with a person's sense of identity. They take over the person's whole life. Although the addiction focuses on one behaviour or object, there are always a whole web of other behaviours and associations that create the conditions for it to continue. Some of these will be general but many are likely to be based in specific thought and behaviour patterns built up by the person. For example, the problem drinker may be triggered into a drinking binge by visiting a pub, or drinking alone, or being with certain friends, or by a particular sort of alcohol, or even a food they associate with it.

Addictions have a powerful hold over the person's life. They have often developed over time and have sucked in associations and patterns of lifestyle along the way. Because they are so all consuming, they become the first point of refuge in any crisis, so layers of grieving, disappointment or other unhappiness are added to the earlier factors which may have precipitated the addiction in the first place.

Even when someone has apparently got a grip on an addiction and given it up, there is a strong tendency to relapse. People with histories of alcohol abuse or other addictions often think of themselves as being in remission rather than having recovered. Often addictions run in families. Whether this is physiological or habit based, children of addicts are particularly vulnerable to addiction themselves.

Triggers and Supports

Our mental state is affected by the 'objects' which we give our attention to. This basic premise has been central to the approach of this book, and in the case of compulsive behaviours and addictions it becomes particularly relevant. If we have our minds on certain things, we feel calm and relaxed, whilst other things agitate us, or stimulate us into thinking along particular lines.

In compulsive or addictive behaviours, a particular set of objects, a person, place, or an activity, becomes the focus of attention. Instead of focusing on whatever is distressing, a person becomes caught up in something compelling. This might be something pleasant or distracting, or it might be a worry or unpleasant thought. Whatever it is, it occupies the mind and keeps attention off other things, which are probably more worrying. In this way a kind of self-medication happens.

MOVING INTO ADDICTION

Shifting attention in this way is something which we learn to do. After a time, the particular behaviour becomes a habit. In addiction, the process of distraction itself becomes a source of anxiety. Will the next 'fix' be available? The object is not just a source of distraction in anxious situations, but is craved at other times. The addiction becomes a source of anxiety, which drives the person to seek out more of the same.

Now, the whole thing has become a loop. The behaviour is addictive and may be complicated by chemical addiction and craving. The person chases more of the experiences which will distract them, in order to cope with the anxiety evoked by the addiction.

Addiction may be to one thing, like alcohol, or drugs, or television violence. Often such things are compelling in their impact on the senses and emotions. Sometimes the person may have multiple addictions, using a range of substances or experiences, but may still be caught in similar patterns of response to each of them. For example, they may seek danger in fast cars, wild relationships and dangerous sports, or oblivion in drugs, alcohol and sleep.

TRIGGERS

Some compulsive behaviour is a direct response to stress or pain. At the point when something distressing happens, the senses are on the look out for particular things onto which they can attach. The eye casts around and sees something which can provide a way to escape. For example, the person walks into their house feeling gloomy and spots the television remote controller, and almost without thinking is sitting in front of the television. Another person walks past the newsagents and recalls that they sell chocolate, and without thinking has entered and bought a couple of bars.

Compulsive and addictive patterns are strongly focused on objects. These objects are part of a scenario which contains many objects. For example, alcohol may be the object of a person's addiction, but the drink is associated with a whole collection of associated objects which includes, maybe a pub or bar, drinking companions, and maybe even particular clothes, food, or enter-tainment. One common problem in escaping an addiction is that for the addict, life becomes centred on the object of the addiction, so everything which is encountered becomes a reminder of the craving.

The situation in which the person takes the first drink is often conditioned by objects which are part of the wider scene, rather than the sight of a bottle of alcohol itself. The pattern of drinking may well start with the process of dressing for an evening out. This means that a behaviour, which might have started as a means of regulating stress, becomes a habit. This in turn might be triggered by things which seem completely stress free, like going out with friends. Relaxing without falling back into the addiction becomes difficult, and, of course, the stress which arises from this makes the person all the more vulnerable to addictive behaviours.

It also means that if you are helping someone to face their compulsive habits you may need to look at what happened before they started drinking. It is common for those working with addictions to help a person to identify objects which act as triggers for addictive behaviour.

People with addiction problems often recognise this sort of pattern all too well; the seemingly innocent action or sight leads to another binge. Whether it is alcohol or drugs, food or gambling, something small is often the trigger for each episode. It might be having money in hand, it might be a sociable outing with friends or it might be a particular place or company.

POSITIVE TRIGGERS

Some ways of distracting ourselves from stress or anxiety are healthier than others. Although the ideal may be to face whatever is happening in our lives without resorting to distractions, realistically it is better to find a healthy way to regulate our feelings than to stay hooked by an unhealthy one. This might mean that rather than drinking to excess, a person gets in the habit of going out to walk in a nearby park when it all gets too much. It might mean sucking sweets rather than smoking.

Making such changes can rely on changing the triggers so that we are reminded to take positive rather than destructive patterns of behaviour. Creating positive triggers, which will lead to positive habit patterns, can be done in a deliberate way. Sowing such seeds will help a person to face stressful situations more positively. Going for a walk in nature or listening to a calm piece of music, learning grounding methods or talking with a friend you trust might all be ways to build good habits.

These good habits create conditions which, in turn, support the more peaceful side of our nature and that will support us in difficult times. Just as the trip to the pub might build a raft of associations which condition a drinking binge, so too, by going to a restaurant with friends instead, the person with a drink problem might condition an evening of conversation in which they do not drink alcohol.

Because the concept of building positive triggers rather than negative ones is so simple, it is one which you might share with people whom you work with. People can often identify things which they find restful and peace-giving and with encouragement will bring them into their regular lives.

Creating positive triggers often involves touching the inspirational. It might include a spiritual practice, if the person has one, or creating opportunities for contact with nature or with art. It often involves finding silence or calm in the midst of a noisy life.

EXERCISE FIVE: CREATING POSITIVE CONDITIONS
(five minutes)

Think about things which you find calming or which put you into a happier, more caring state of mind.

How much do you currently incorporate these things into your regular life?

Are these things which you might use to create positive triggers at times of stress?

Some people, however, find it difficult to face quiet or beauty. For the person who is in distress, silence may be unbearable because it contains nothing to distract. Focusing on the body in grounding exercises may feel overwhelming because the body is so wracked with grief or anxiety that the person cannot bear to experience it.

For such people, more active responses to distress can be helpful.

Tackling an addiction is not easy. As a listener, you are not likely to be the sole supporter of an addict, but you may well find people with addiction problems using your agency. It is worth bearing in mind a few strategies that may help the person who is trying to break such a habit so that you can suggest possible approaches or support the person when they seem to be following them naturally:

- Talk about stress or grief before it builds up.
- Be aware of the triggers which start the addictive behaviour.
- Be aware of the circumstances or environments in which the behaviour happens.
- Find 'positive triggers' which replace the habitual ones.
- Help the person to find support from people who are not similarly addicted.
- Help the person discover meaning in life so that they can make sense of the painful things which happen.
- Help them to find a sense of purpose.

Three Stages

The process of distraction which we have been describing can be seen as having three stages. The first stage involves using sensory experiences as distractions from the problem. The second stage involves the repetition of these patterns of distraction to the point where they become the basis of our sense of identity.

In this session we have already looked at the way that people move from sensory distractions into identification. This process is particularly clear with addictive patterns, as the distraction, which began simply as a way for the person to take the mind off a stressful situation, takes over that person's life and becomes their whole identity and reason for living.

There is a third stage beyond this, in which the sense of identity no longer provides a distraction from painful feelings, and indeed, has perhaps itself been damaged by an experience of loss or dislocation from the foundations of the person's life. This third stage is one of self-destructiveness.

SENSORY DISTRACTIONS	IDENTITY CREATION	SELF-DESTRUCTION

The last stage of self-destruction is a time in which the person just wants to find oblivion. It can be the final part of an addictive process. Watching someone intent on self-destruction is very distressing. Such a person becomes very cut off from other people, so that anything which you, as listener, can do to gain personal contact with them will be helpful. It may help bring the person out of the pit of destructiveness into which they have fallen, and restore their will to continue their life. Since this stage is the stage which occurs when the craving for identity has been abandoned, supporting things which re-establish a sense of self may also be helpful.

Although one might hope that a person who has reached this point of desperation would receive the help of the full range of professional services, often such a person is very hard to work with and they may have exhausted the net of social support long ago. For this reason, such a person may well end up receiving whatever help they get from grass roots voluntary sector organisations.

This is, in fact, often the most appropriate form of help that such a person can receive. They may well be living rough or in transient conditions and only able to relate to others in limited ways, so small doses of everyday interaction and ordinary kindness may help them to crawl back to a point where they can start to engage with life again.

MEDITATION EXERCISE

Sit in your quiet space and observe your breathing.

As you sit, thoughts and impulses may arise. Notice when this happens, but do not let yourself become caught up in them. With each thought breathe out and bring your attention back to your breathing.

Continue to observe the stream of breath and the activity of thoughts as they pass through your mind. You can think of this process as being like sitting on a river bank, watching the water flow past you. You do not need to jump in. You can just observe it.

Enjoy the feeling of calm that arises as you sit.

Afterwards create a picture of your mind during the meditation using pens, paint or collage

Session Twelve

Good Faith

This session will include:

- Faith and Trust
- Carl Rogers and the self-actualising tendency
- Gisho Saiko's theory of faith
- Faith and Beliefs
- Grounding our faith
- Silence
- Endings

Faith and Trust

Listening to others is a great privilege. When we listen to people's stories, we are often trusted with things which the person might only tell to those most intimately involved in their life. Sometimes they share things they have not told anyone for years, or never told anyone before.

Offering a listening space to people is an act of faith. We are venturing into the unknown. We do not know what they will tell us. We do not know if we have the capacity to receive it or to act accordingly. We do not know if we will be able to help. We do not know if it will disturb us by reminding us of painful things in our own lives. We do not know if it will compel us to take some action. We do not know what sort of relationship we will have with the person, or even if we will be physically safe with the person. We may assess risks and make judgements about what is the right thing to do, but within these parameters we still have to trust the other person and, if we are to have a working relationship, they have to come to trust us.

In as much as we do trust one another, we show faith.

- In listening, we show faith that it is good for the person to speak because we give them the space to talk freely.
- They show faith in us by trusting us with sensitive information about their life and feelings and intuitions that they hold.
- We both show faith in the process of listening as a source of healing and support.

TRUSTING THE PROCESS

As we spend time with people who are distressed, we gradually gain confidence as listeners. This takes time because we need to build up experience. We need to see people helped by the listening process, and see their lives improving. In this way, the listener sees that the process of listening works, and that what they are able to offer will usually help others.

More globally, the listener sees how time and again, people who seem to be in impossible situations, make good against the odds. Time heals and the human spirit resurfaces in even the most dreadful calamities.

The Self Actualising Tendency

Seeing the way that positive outcomes often emerge when a situation seems most difficult, the listener gains confidence, not just in the listening process, but also in a wider beneficence to be found in the life process itself. Carl Rogers, the well know psychologist whom we referred to earlier, called this process *the self-actualising tendency*.

Rogers told a story about how, as a child, he had gone down into a cellar and found an old sack of potatoes which had started to sprout. He was fascinated by the way that, despite the dreadful conditions, these shrivelled vegetables had put out shoots which twisted in a tangled mass towards the light. Even in these poorest of conditions, where there was almost no nutrient or water available to them and where the light was faint, the life energy was still asserting itself. Even here growth happened.

The story of the potatoes became an inspiration not only to Rogers, but also to the many counsellors, educators and other workers who adopted his ideas and methods. The possibility that there was a force in the universe which grew towards the light and that the human psyche naturally grew towards health became an underpinning dogma of the person-centred approach.

In addition to this, Rogers came to believe that growth happened in an optimal way when certain basic conditions were offered. In session nine we saw how these were formulated as *the core conditions*.

Rogers' theory does not dictate that everything will get better. It does not say that everyone will become psychologically healthy, even with the best conditions. What it postulates is a bias; a tendency in the universe and in the human psyche towards wholeness and towards healing.

Whether or not Rogers was objectively right, the idea of the self-actualising tendency has been a potent force, inspiring generations of people working with the unhappy and the disturbed. Theories are both testable hypotheses and catalysts which affect the thinking of their adherents. The fact that the theory postulated an optimistic view of the human condition inspired people to be optimistic about the people they met and this, no doubt, inspired them to optimise their lives. Thus, the theory, if nothing else, became a self-fulfilling prophesy.

Beyond this, however, the theory does describe a human spirit which many will recognise. Those of us who have spent years supporting and listening to people in distress will recall many instances of remarkable people who lived fruitful lives despite dreadful conditions. Such people are an inspiration to us in continuing our work.

EXERCISE ONE: THE SELF-ACTUALISING TENDENCY

(five minutes)

Reflect on Rogers' image of the potatoes. Are there experiences which you have had which have stayed with you in similar ways and which have inspired you?

What do you take from Rogers' theory of the self-actualising tendency? Is it something which you observe in your work?

Gisho Saiko

A Japanese Psychologist called Gisho Saiko was inspired by Rogers. Saiko developed his own theory, which is also about the underpinning of faith which is brought into the listening situation and which is the source of healing.

In some ways Saiko's theory echoes Rogers' belief in the self-actualising tendency. He sees the encounter between counsellor and client, listener and service user, as resting on a basic faith in a greater process which holds both parties and supports the unfolding of healing in their meeting. For Saiko, faith is an explicit element in the process. It is not just a healing tendency which effects change, but rather, it is the therapist or listener's *faith* in a supportive presence, which makes the difference.

According to Saiko, at the start of the relationship there is a meeting of the two people, but only the listener has faith. The other person who is coming to talk about their troubles does not. Indeed, their seeking out of a listener might be seen as a sort of failure of faith in a universal source of support (though it might also be seen as evidence of a latent faith that healing is possible).

So the listener's faith supports the person who is in distress even when that person does not have faith herself. Eventually this person will come to trust life more through 'catching' the therapist's faith.

Saiko represented his theory through a diagram. This diagram is made up of two overlapping triangles. The one representing the listener is continuous, whereas the other has a broken line in its lower portion. There is a line which demarcates the division between conscious and unconscious process. Above the line, the two people meet, representing the fact that the listener and the person being supported are in psychological contact. This is the open, conscious encounter which happens in the session.

Below the line, the listener's triangle is solid. This represents the listener's confidence in the healing process and in the healing resources available to them. It also represents the fact that this confidence extends under the whole psychological space of the encounter. It underpins both participants in the meeting.

The person who is seeking help, meanwhile, has only has a faint, broken line in the lower part of her triangle. This represents a potential for faith but shows that the faith is not yet present. The person is permeable to the listener's faith and is held by it. Her faith needs to be held and supported by the listener's faith.

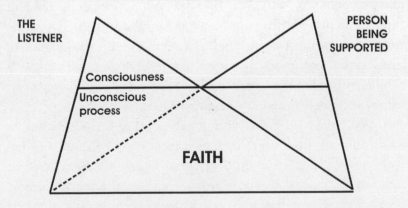

Because Saiko was religious, in his theory the underpinning force which is the focus of the listener's faith is the *measureless* presence of light and love. We can, therefore, think of the underpinning quality as being the spiritual dimension; the love that is available in the universe, or the ever-present potential for people to move towards wholeness.

While Rogers sees the source of healing as being within the client, Saiko's model sees the source of support as being beyond either listener or the person being helped. The deep source of support in Saiko's model is not within the practitioner, but is a separate presence which is pictured as beneath the relationship, upholding it. It is to be related to. It is *other*. So, according to Saiko's model, the quality that heals us is not something which we have to discover within ourselves, but something universal which is external to us and upon which we can rely.

This theory of a reliable presence which underpins life, and which does not require us to find all the resources within ourselves, can be a source of inspiration to the listener. Once more, it is helpful not just in its accuracy or otherwise, but also in the effect which it can have on the person using it.

THE ROLE OF FAITH AND RELIGIOUS VIEWS

Saiko's theory shows how a religious idea can be incorporated into psychological work, bringing the faith dimension to life and showing that there need not be a hard and fast line between the psychological theory and the religious one. Clearly there are issues about not imposing views or proselytising to vulnerable people, but, at the same time, no psychological theory is free from values and dogmas about the human situation.

If you have a religious faith, it is helpful to consider what its implications are for your work as a listener. How does it shape your view of people and influence your work with them? Does it facilitate it or does it impose restrictions on it? Does it support people equally whether they are of the same faith or a different one and does it help them to grow in their own faith?

The language in which a theory is expressed can make a difference to the way that it is perceived. Religious theory can often be expressed in secular language and vice versa. The important thing is whether it conveys a message which is conducive to the work which you are doing. For a secular audience, Saiko's ideas were presented in forums where they were compared to those of Rogers'. For his own followers, Saiko had no hesitation in using more religious language because this was a language which they understood.

EXERCISE TWO: COMPARING ROGERS AND SAIKO

(twenty-five minutes)

Compare your responses to the models offered by Rogers and by Saiko. Which speaks to you most, and why?

How do you think your faith, beliefs or life philosophy influence the way others feel supported by you? Do you have a model in mind which integrates them into your work?

Take a sheet of paper and draw your own model of the relationship between listener and the person being listened to and incorporate into it your sense of the place of faith.

Faith and Beliefs

It is probably useful to make a distinction at this point between faith and beliefs. It has been said that faith is what we have when we don't have beliefs, and beliefs are what we have when we don't have faith. This is a little simplistic since both words can be used in a variety of ways, but there is certainly an opposition between the sort of faith which we are talking about in this session and the sort of belief which is dogmatically clung to.

If by beliefs we mean 'things which we assert', then it may be that we assert them because, at some level, we are uncertain. This may be true whether we believe in a religion, science, a political ideology or whatever. We cling to such beliefs because they represent something which fits our world view. They are rigid because they are linked to our perspective on life and, thus, to our sense of identity, so we are frightened to allow ourselves to consider the possibility that they might be wrong. We need them to be right.

Faith, on the other hand, is the trust we have in something which is beyond our capacity to fully know. It is our willingness to step forth into life experience with trust but without certainties. It is our confidence that even if we come unstuck, there are greater processes at work in the universe than ourselves.

According to these definitions, both faith and beliefs might be religious or might not be. Both are also things which we all have. Our faith is always going to be imperfect because we are human, *bombu*, and we will always try to bridge the gap between faith and doubt with beliefs. These beliefs are not without their usefulness either. They may be the symbols around which our spiritual sense crystallises. They may be the images from which we draw inspiration.

So faith is not necessarily about belief. We can have lots of faith but few actual beliefs. It takes faith to live confidently without 'knowing' all the answers to life questions. Although they are linked, 'having faith' and 'holding beliefs' are not necessarily the same thing.

Grounding Our Faith

The faith which we bring to our work is grounded in our life philosophy and our spiritual beliefs. Whether or not we are religious, the way we see the world affects what we offer to others. It creates the container for our work, and underlies our responses, even though we are unlikely to speak of it directly.

This is because our belief system affects the whole way in which we approach life; our confidence in life, our level of concern for other people, our moral outlook, our energy, our attitudes towards others. Others will sense our attitudes and our level of faith even when we do not talk about it. Indeed, when we do not talk about it, they may sense it most strongly.

Belief systems vary of course. Some make people more humble, others make them arrogant; some give them an optimistic outlook, others make them fearful or gloomy. We are talking here about both organised religions and more generalised life philosophies. In all cases, we are probably aware of some of the ways our beliefs about life affect our outlook, but we probably also have many blind spots. When we listen, we offer ourselves to others. Our responses come not just from techniques and skills we have learned, but also from who we are and, most importantly, what quality of faith is apparent in us.

Trust

The trust which the people whom we are supporting put in us is a kind of faith. It is always remarkable just how willing most people are to trust strangers. They talk to someone in a listening role about their life, their hopes, their struggles and the intimate details of their thoughts, often when they have only just met them.

At the same time, most people do go through a process of testing out and trusting by degrees. Although they may initially tell you a great deal about their situation, probably there will be some things which are held back and only shared if the person feels that the listener is really trustworthy.

This process of testing out is subtle and often unconscious. Mostly the person is not consciously deciding whether to trust you or not, but, rather, is getting a feel for what is possible in the relationship. As you probably discovered if you did exercise six in session four, some things just feel more possible with one person and other things feel possible with someone else.

Sometimes people test out the trustworthiness of a listener through their behaviour. They may do something which at some level they know will push the limits of what is acceptable to the listener in order to see how the listener reacts. Recall the things which you identified as triggers which might lead you to be judgemental in exercise nine of session nine. Do you think some of these things might be said to test you out? Again, this sort of provocation is probably not something done with a conscious intention of testing the listener, but, depending on how you respond, it probably strengthens or compromises the relationship.

If you suspect someone is testing out whether they can trust you, in most cases the best response is just to take the behaviour on face value and respond in a caring, but, if necessary, firm way. Be wary of breaking boundaries which you would normally keep. Discuss the matter with someone in a supervisory role if you can.

Things someone might do to test out whether they could trust you might include:
- Arriving late
- Telling you something personal or shocking to see your reaction
- Asking to borrow something
- Wanting extra sessions or meetings
- Flirting
- Getting angry with you
- Being off hand
- Missing appointments

EXERCISE THREE: TESTING TRUST
(five minutes)

Reflect on your experiences of trusting people. Have you ever done any of the things listed above as a way of testing trust? Were you aware of doing it? What was the response?

Have you experienced other people behaving in any of these ways with you? How did you respond? Do you think your response was skilful? How else might you have responded?

Silence

We tend to think of being a listener as being about sharing a conversation, but sometimes the listener and the person whom they are supporting will spend periods of time sitting together in silence. It may be that the person talking is overwhelmed with emotion. It may be that they are sick and do not have the energy to speak. It may be that they have run out of things to say. It may be they are thinking so hard that they have not realised that they have stopped talking. It may be that what they are feeling does not need to be put into words.

Some people feel very uncomfortable with silences and feel a pressure to break in and say something, but if you are a listener, this may be completely wrong. It may be very important to give the person space to be quiet and reflective or to struggle to find the right words. Becoming comfortable with silence is an important aspect of learning to listen.

We often sense another person's life stance in their quality of presence. This can be felt as much in silence as in communication. Sometimes the connection which we feel to someone in a shared silence can be far deeper than anything we feel when talking.

Silence can have many different qualities. It can be:
- Scary
- Intense
- Boring
- Romantic
- Thoughtful
- Embarrassing
- Peaceful

Learning to be comfortable with silence is, then, an important skill. Sitting in silence, we learn to sense the other person in new ways. A lot is communicated without words. Silence helps us to listen with our eyes and with our bodies, not just our ears.

EXERCISE FOUR: EXPLORING SILENCE
(twenty minutes)

If you are in a group, do this exercise in pairs to explore your experience of silence:

Sit opposite your partner in silence for five minutes. Give your partner the best attention you can. After you have finished, share your experience:
- What was the experience like?
- What did you notice?
- What do you think your partner was feeling or thinking?
- Did you notice this changing over the session?
- Did you make eye contact? If so, what happened?
- Did you notice thoughts or images or feelings coming up in you?

What was the process of sharing like? Did you discover ways in which you had observed things in your partner that he/she then confirmed? Were there things you were 'wrong' about?

If you are reading this on your own, recall times when you have sat with people in silence. Reflect on the quality of the silence.
- What do you think it was about?
- How comfortable did you feel in the silence?

If you do not recall any such situations, try to observe yourself over the next week when you are with people. What do you do if it looks as if a silence might arise? Try remaining silent and see what happens.

Endings

In listening relationships, the ending is not always clear cut. In many situations, users come and go, and you do not know that someone has moved on until you realise that you have not seen them for a time. Sometimes, however, endings are planned. Sometimes there is a befriending arrangement which has a limited duration. Sometimes you are working with people in a group and the group is due to come to an end. Sometimes you are, yourself, due to move on from a particular agency.

Where there is a planned ending, or where an ending is foreseen, perhaps because someone is moving away from the area, this can provide opportunities to reflect on the process of ending.

Endings can be difficult times for some people. Whether it is the end of a group or the end of a supportive relationship, saying good-bye is not always easy. Sometimes, for some people it can even be difficult to know how to actually finish. Sometimes the ending brings up memories of other endings or partings, or it can remind people of fears which they have about losing loved ones or being alone.

If you have been supporting someone for a while and a clear cut ending is in sight, it can be valuable to give time to talk about that ending and to say goodbye properly. You may use the time for:

- Reflecting back over the time you have been together and looking at the good points and maybe the not so good ones.
- Dealing with unfinished business, things which got glossed over or loose ends.
- Marking the ending, maybe by doing something special together or creating some sort of reminder together of the work you have done.
- Talking about any feelings of loss or memories the ending has evoked.
- Looking at ways forward: hopes, fears and plans for the future.
- Looking at any future support needs and how they can be met.
- Making sure the person has a good support network.
- Deciding what contact, if any, you will have in the future

There are also pitfalls to be aware of around endings:

- Be aware of the tendency to gloss over endings or avoid saying goodbye. As we saw in session ten, facing the reality of our losses and partings is much healthier, and facing the ending of a helping relationship can be a good way to learn new habits of not avoiding endings.
- Be careful to keep boundaries up to the end. There can be a temptation to relax and try to become friends in the last session but this often does not work. Do not agree to things you cannot

fulfil. Be wary of accepting large gifts (though something simple like a bunch of flowers or box of chocolates may be fine). Be aware that inappropriately large gifts may be part of the other person's attempt to ward off the feelings they have about ending.

- Leave things in a way that allows you to offer more help in future if this fits with the circumstances.

EXERCISE FIVE: HANDLING ENDINGS
(five minutes)

Think about the setting in which you practice listening. Do you go through an ending process with people or do they just come and go in a casual way?

If you do have a foreseeable end point, how do you handle it? Use the points above as a checklist and see how they compare with your experience. Are there things which you would like to improve?

If you do not have formal endings, are there times when people leave your agency which could be marked more effectively?

When you have experienced endings yourself as a service user, what needs have you had?

Make notes on your reflections.

Reflecting Back

As we reach the end of this book, you may wish to reflect back over what we have done.

Ending is a time for looking back and for looking forward. This book has taken you through some of the important areas of reflection in developing your skills as a listener. It has done this through practical exercises and guidance on method, but it has also done it by inviting you to look at some of the attitudes and values which you might bring to the work, which inevitably underpin what you offer and the way that you offer it.

EXERCISE SIX: REVIEWING YOUR LEARNING
(as long as you wish)

Think back through the topics you have covered in this book.

What learning stands out for you?

Have you already used any skills or knowledge which you have acquired in your work or volunteering?

Where do you go from here? What is your next step?

It may be that for you listening is part of your professional work, a skill which you are developing to complement other aspects of a rounded career. It may be that you listen as a volunteer or in your church or community centre. It may be that this is a first step towards learning counselling skills, or indeed that you are a counsellor looking for a new approach. Whatever your reason for reading this book, I hope that you have found it helpful.

Whatever your background and intention, there will always be more to learn. Learning is part of being human and whether or not it leads to qualifications, is what breathes life into us. If you are working with people, you will learn a great deal from them. In all the years that I have been using listening or counselling skills, I have been deeply indebted to so many amazing people who have freely shared their stories with me.

At the same time, it may be that through reading this book you have become interested in developing your skills further in a formal way. Now may be a time to look forward and identify another step along the road.

Being a listener is not really about skills. Skills can be developed and there is plenty of theory and methodology to learn. More importantly, though, listening is about you and the qualities which you bring to the work. When you sit down with someone, what you offer to them is not a package, taken off the shelf and delivered to them in some professional way. It is you who listens and it is your humanity, your ordinariness, your caring concern and your faith which you offer. That is the most precious gift in the world.

MEDITATION

Return to your quiet space and spend a few minutes grounding yourself. Be aware of your body making contact with the floor or chair on which you are seated. Be aware of the air which you are breathing and the light that bathes you.

Breathe softly and hear your breath amid the noises of the world. Feel your breath flowing between the layers of sound and silence, reaching out, receiving. Smile.

Hold in your thoughts the processes which you have experienced as you have gone through this book. Recall the people you have reflected on and those whom you have met in actuality. Send thoughts of appreciation and kindliness to them.

Hold in your thoughts the people who are in your life at present. Recall those whom you listen to and those whom maybe you do not hear as well as you might. Send thoughts of appreciation and kindliness to them.

Hold in your thoughts the people who you will meet in the future. Think of those to whom you will offer a listening ear or a strong shoulder on which to cry. Think of those who will inspire you and those who maybe will be inspired by you. Send thoughts of appreciation and kindliness to them.

Then send your thoughts out to the planet, to the universe, to the great web of life and love which holds us all. Breathe and bask in that love.

End Notes

Orientation

This book is a practical introduction, aimed at anyone who needs or wishes to develop their capacity to listen. It is also a useful foundation for those who wish to go on to learn counselling skills. Because of this practical orientation, I have avoided using jargon or going into theory in any depth.

The underpinning theory of the approach is the same as that used on courses in the Amida training programme in counselling and psychotherapy, and is grounded in the models offered by Buddhist theory of mental conditioning. This is an approach which particularly suits community and activity-based settings. It sees the person as immersed in and conditioned by their environment and the people around them. It emphasises an outward focus in which exploration of the reality of experience takes precedence over mulling on feelings and personal perspectives, though the exploration of the latter has its place. It emphasises relationship and honesty, appreciation and respect for difference.

This theory differs from many other approaches to listening in its radical focus on the *others*, whether people, places or objects, which create the net of conditions for the person, but its methods are very compatible with and complementary to Western approaches and methodologies.

If you would like to know more about this orientation, you will find that there is full presentation of the theory of conditioning, including concepts such as *association* and *object relation*, in David Brazier's book, *Zen Therapy* (Constable Robinson. 1995) whilst the discussion of loss and the teaching of the Four Noble Truths is explored in *The Feeling Buddha* (Constable Robinson. 1997). The models which integrate these theories with those of *Dependent Origination, Four Noble Truths* and the cycle of conditioned perception are all presented in my earlier book, *Buddhist Psychology* (Constable Robinson. 2003).

Ideas about ordinary, bombu nature, getting beyond guilt, and the importance of faith in mental health, are presented in my book, *The Other Buddhism* (O-Books. 2007). These are also addressed in my new book, *Guilt* (O-Books. 2009). You can read a good introduction to *Naikan* therapy in Gregg Krech's book *Naikan: gratitude, grace, and the Japanese art of self-reflection* (Stonebridge Press 2001). To read more on Carl Rogers' work you may refer to any of his books, but particularly *On Becoming a Person* (Constable Robinson. 1961). David's book, *Who Loves Dies well* (O-Books. 2007) deals with spiritual issues and the accompaniment of the dying.

If you wish to find out more about the Amida Training Programmes, you will find details on the Amida website at www.buddhistpsychology.info, or you can write to us at:
Amida Trust
The Buddhist House
12 Coventry Rd
Narborough
LE19 2GR UK

BOOKS

O is a symbol of the world, of oneness and unity. In different cultures it also means the "eye," symbolizing knowledge and insight. We aim to publish books that are accessible, constructive and that challenge accepted opinion, both that of academia and the "moral majority."

Our books are available in all good English language bookstores worldwide. If you don't see the book on the shelves ask the bookstore to order it for you, quoting the ISBN number and title. Alternatively you can order online (all major online retail sites carry our titles) or contact the distributor in the relevant country, listed on the copyright page.

See our website **www.o-books.net** for a full list of over 500 titles, growing by 100 a year.

And tune in to myspiritradio.com for our book review radio show, hosted by June-Elleni Laine, where you can listen to the authors discussing their books.

MySpiritRadio